RELIGION AND THE
RISE OF MODERN SCIENCE

RELIGION AND THE RISE OF MODERN SCIENCE

By

R. HOOYKAAS

*Professor of the History of Science
in the University of Utrecht*

1972
SCOTTISH ACADEMIC PRESS
EDINBURGH AND LONDON

Published by
Scottish Academic Press Ltd
25 Perth Street, Edinburgh, 3
and distributed by
Chatto & Windus Ltd
40 William IV Street
London W.C.2

ISBN 7011 1835 0

© Professor R. Hooykaas 1972

Printed in Great Britain by R. & R. Clark, Ltd., Edinburgh

CONTENTS

Contents

Contents

To the Memory of
Janet C. MacKay
1892–1964

ACKNOWLEDGEMENTS

The Gunning Lectures on which this book is based were delivered under the auspices of the Faculty of Divinity in the University of Edinburgh, in February 1969.

My feelings of apprehension at this, the first close contact in a long career with a theological faculty, were pleasantly dispelled. In effect the old tradition which Fleming and Miller bequeathed to New College had left its mark in a lively awareness of the continuing need to clarify the relations between religious and scientific thought.

I owe a special debt of gratitude to Principal McIntyre and to Mr. David Wright for all they did to make my stay both comfortable and profitable, and to Professor Torrance for giving freely of his time to the discussion of many topics of mutual interest.

In bringing this book to its present form the assistance of Professor D. M. MacKay, Mr. Douglas Grant and the staff of the Scottish Academic Press has been invaluable.

R. HOOYKAAS

INTRODUCTION

The essential revolution in scientific thought took place in the sixteenth and seventeenth centuries. However great a change there may have been in our own time, Planck, Einstein and Bohr did not make Newtonian science obsolete, whereas the classical-modern science built up from Copernicus to Newton made most of ancient and medieval science null and void.

This statement poses the question why modern science arose in a particular place, in Europe, and at a particular time, and not elsewhere or in a different age. It is generally acknowledged that we owe to the Greeks, if not the special tenets, at least the general mental tools of our science. Whatever the sixteenth and seventeenth centuries may have rejected of the ancient scientific heritage, they continued to use parts of it—logic, mathematics and experimentation.

That other root of European civilization, the Judaeo-Christian, finds less positive appreciation. Current opinion would hold that science grew thanks to the classical and in spite of the biblical tradition. Even theologians and clergymen sometimes show great zeal in disavowing the ecclesiastical past and in deploring the retarding influence of the church on the development of science. The role played by Bible exegesis in offering resistance to new scientific theories on the movement of the earth, the age of the earth and the origin of animal species has been emphasized again and again. However, just as it would be wrong to blame Aristotle for all prejudiced, dogmatic and even silly interpretations of his philosophy put forward by his scholastic followers, so it would be wrong to lay to the account of the biblical authors the shortsighted interpretations of those who used the work of these authors to oppose scientific opinions and discoveries. Moreover, quarrels about the allegedly scientific content of Bible texts were incidents which did not affect the development of science at all places or at all times.

On the other hand, a more penetrating enquiry shows that there is an essential difference between the cultural legacies of the Greeks and those of the Bible. The Greeks possessed an elaborate scientific world picture and they laid the foundations of some scientific disciplines, such as astronomy and optics. The Bible, on the contrary, builds up no world picture and contains no scientific data which could serve as a basis for a further development. Consequently, the Hebrews made even fewer contributions of lasting value to the material content of our sciences than did the Greeks. Nevertheless, since the main legacy of the Greeks is to be found not in their particular theories but in the general attitude they left us (an attitude of rational investigation of nature by means of logic, mathematics and observation), one could ask whether the same might not also be said of the biblical influence. Might not the world *view* found in the Bible, if not the world *picture*, have had a lasting positive influence on science? It seems hardly credible that, whereas European thought has been profoundly influenced by both Graeco-Roman and biblical sources, only the former should have set their stamp on our way of scientific thinking. Until the scientific revolution of the sixteenth and seventeenth centuries, however, the contents and methods of science did not differ essentially from those of antiquity. Although some of the first Christians wholly rejected Greek philosophy and science, others went far in seeking a compromise, without finding new ways. The beginning of the science of the Christian epoch was similar to the end of that of the declining pagan era.

In the Middle Ages the Bible was to a large extent read through 'Greek' spectacles, and often the result was an uneasy compromise. It could hardly be said that Christian theology had a purifying or fertilizing influence on the classical heritage. Medieval science made no move to eliminate the main shortcomings inherent in the Greek approach to nature, for we find again the same under-estimation of human power and the deification of nature; the over-estimation of human reason; and the under-valuing of manual work.

This raises the question whether the correctives later found for these weaknesses—namely a 'de-deification' of nature, a more modest estimation of human reason, and a higher respect for manual labour—were perhaps latent in neglected aspects of the biblical tradition. If so, we ought to be able to identify some general trends of thought in the Bible which could exert a healthy influence on the development of science, and it might be that in the sixteenth and seventeenth centuries these managed to overcome the shortcomings of the Greek attitude.

Of course religion, though an important factor in creating the spiritual climate of thought, is not the only one. External influences, whether social, economic, political or geographic, and internal ones such as philosophy or ethics, also play their part. The situation is made more complex because these factors are interrelated; religious and social conceptions, for example, are closely intertwined. But in the epoch when modern science arose religion was one of the most powerful factors in cultural life. What people thought about God (or the gods) influenced their conception of nature, and this in turn influenced their method of investigating nature, that is their science.

In the following lectures we shall investigate how far

Greek and biblical factors played a part in creating a certain attitude to nature. This we shall do by comparing the Greek and biblical concepts of God and nature, and the scientific methodologies that ensued from these concepts, with special reference to the scope and limitations of human reason (rationalism and empiricism), human power (the limits of nature and art), and the role of head and hand in the investigation of nature.

CHAPTER I

GOD AND NATURE

A. THE GREEK VIEW

a. *The Pre-Socratics*

To the ancient Greek *theologoi*, cosmogony and theogony were closely connected; the gods personified cosmic powers resulting from processes of love and generation. The world was a living organism, the divine source of all living beings, the gods included. Though the Ionian *physikoi* depersonalized the myths, the fundamental idea remained the same. *Physis* was to them mainly the process of coming-to-be and growth of all things; it meant practically the same as genesis. 'Matter' had become the divine Being itself, which worked in it and was one with it.[1] Thales (sixth century B.C.) considered water to be the origin of all things, and according to Aristotle the ancients said the same in a mythological way when they called Okeanos and Tethys the origins of the world.[2] There is a story that Herakleitos, who considered fire to be the origin of all things, would stand near the kitchen fire and welcome his guests with the words: 'Come in, here too there are gods'. These philosophers looked on nature herself as the deity, an eternal being continuously regenerating itself. Sometimes it was identified by them with the Olympic gods. In this way these gods, who derived from the spirits that animated trees and lakes and rivers, re-assumed their original character in a rationalized form. As Aeschylus put it: 'Zeus is the aether, Zeus the earth, the heaven is Zeus, Zeus is all and all that is above it'. So 'philosophy may have been the death of the ancient gods, but it was itself a religion.'[3]

I

After the Eleatic philosophers (fifth century B.C.) had demonstrated that the divine being must be absolutely without any change, the later philosophers of nature set themselves the task of 'saving the phenomena'. While maintaining the immutability of true being, they tried at the same time to explain apparent changes in the world of phenomena by the rearrangement, separation and union of small unalterable particles. Empedocles' four elements (earth, water, air, fire) bore the names of Olympic gods; their union by the force of love (Aphrodite) brought forth all things, the sun, the earth, the trees and even the 'long-living gods'.[4]

The atomists, when they rejected any rational principle in nature, stayed in this respect outside the religious tradition of the natural philosophers. Nevertheless they remained within it when they deified nature almost as much as their predecessors. The atomists, too, recognized the unchangeability of true being, but, like Empedocles, they advocated a philosophical polytheism instead of the Eleatic philosophical monotheism; they postulated an infinite number of indivisible and unalterable atoms, of an infinite variety of sizes and shapes, moving in an infinite empty space. Phenomena were saved by reducing all apparent change to local change, to the separation or the rearrangement of these atoms. Here the divine being is pulverized into atoms, but these bear unmistakably divine attributes; they are eternal, unchangeable, self-sufficient. The atomists felt that all things happen according to the law of Necessity. This Necessity, however, is an efficient cause, resting in the inherent properties of the atoms, and not a final one, not a plan.

Nevertheless, in this Necessity we meet again a vestige of the old religion, which recognized that *moira* (fate), *ananke* (necessity), *dike* (justice), are all aspects of a universal world order, which even the gods cannot violate without incurring retribution.[5] According to Herakleitos the sun remains within the bounds allotted to him, because otherwise the Furies, the servants of *dike* (justice), will find him.[6] Necessity (*ananke*), then, is as it were a super-god, the moral order of nature, to which not only the Olympic gods or the nature-gods of the philosophers, but even the atom-gods have to submit. However widely diverging the different conceptions of the pre-socratic philosophers may have been, yet, as O. Gilbert put it: 'all Ionian and Eleatic, and even Pythagorean speculation, is nothing but the search for the godhead: that is, for the divine substance that determines and supports the development of the world'.[7]

b. *Plato*

Plato (429–348) had been strongly influenced by the Eleatics; he considered that absolutely immutable Ideas form the real world, of which the visible world of phenomena and change is but a shadowy image. Knowledge is proportional to the degree of true being of its subject; what being is to becoming (coming-to-be), truth is to opinion (*doxa*). 'Ideas' are the eternal models of which the multiplicity of visible things are, so to speak, the distorted, and not wholly real, images.

In his *Timaios* Plato gives an account of the origin of the visible world. The *demiourgos*, a personal 'creator', shaped the world according to a definite plan. But his hands were tied in two respects: he had to follow not his own design but the model of the eternal Ideas; and secondly, he had to put the stamp of the Ideas on a chaotic, recalcitrant matter which he had not created himself. He was a regulating power bringing reason into reason-less matter,[8] rather than a Creator in the biblical sense. He could make nothing but

imitations of Ideas, and he could not even do this in a perfect way, as matter, standing over against him, offered
resistance.

It is difficult to assign to the demiurge the right place in
the Platonic hierarchy. Perhaps he was the mythical personification of the supreme Idea of the Good. In that case
the history of the origin of the world would be but a
chronological translation of a purely ontological relation,
and the demiurge would stand for the Ideas. Thus it becomes
understandable why he is said to have made the earth, the
heavens and the gods, 'himself included'.[9] There are here
great obstacles to interpretation, as Plato himself recognized
when he said: 'To find the maker and father of this universe
is very difficult.'[10]

The visible universe itself was considered by Plato to be
also a divine being, the image of the highest God, the realm
of Ideas. Within this divine universe 'the heavenly tribe of
the gods'—the stars, the sun, the moon and the earth—are
'the visible and created gods'. In other dialogues these bodies
bear the names of Olympic gods (Zeus was the equivalent
of the heaven of the fixed stars, Hestia was the earth)[11] who,
though not essentially immortal, would never be subject
to disintegration. As the creation of mortal beings by the
eternal God would be impossible, these 'created gods' have
the task of forming the bodies of men and animals, although
their souls were given by the highest God himself.

Plato rejected the sophists' concept of the blind necessity
of nature (*ananke physeos*). The visible things, which his
opponents called *physis*, come only in the second place; they
are themselves products of Intellect and Design. Accordingly Plato used the term *physis* for the world soul (the
moving and animating principle of the universe) as well as
for the Ideas and even for the stars, It should be remembered

4

that all these entities were considered to be 'divine'. That is to say, in spite of a different emphasis, he continued the ancient Greek tradition when he made *physis*, the world intellect, an eternal god.

c. *Aristotle*

Aristotle (384–322) shifted the emphasis towards the world of visible things. For him the world of Ideas (or Forms, as he called them) coincides with the visible world. The spherical universe has a movement of rotation; its centre is occupied by the immovable earth. There is an essential difference between the supra-lunar world, consisting of *aither* and admitting of no other than circular motions, and the sublunar world of the four elements earth, water, air and fire, where the only *natural* movement is rectilinear, that is either downwards, towards the centre of the world, or upwards, towards the sphere of the moon.

Aristotle's god is the Prime Mover; he is, however, not an efficient cause, but only a final one; he is absorbed in self-contemplation and does not care for the world. The prime mover is not the creator; the world, the Forms (Ideas), matter are all eternal. On the other hand, Aristotle fully recognized that there is change in this sublunar world, which was taken seriously by locating the Forms within it. Individuals might pass away and come into being, but these changes themselves are always the same; the same Forms that have always been, will always exist; individuals may change, but the species remains the same. As the Prime Mover was the highest of Forms (in a similar way to Plato's Idea of the Good), it follows that the immutability of the Prime Mover is shared even by the lower Forms. The essence or Form of a natural thing is the end of its individual development; it is its *physis*, its 'nature'. Physics, then, is the discipline that studies the *physis*, the Form, of each thing and the movements or changes tending towards the full realization of the Forms.

'*Physis*' is also the totality of all Forms in their rational order; it is eternal, unchangeable, uncreated, self-regenerating and rational. Aristotle spoke about nature in an anthropomorphic way. For him nature 'makes things' (*demiourgein*); as he puts it, 'Nature makes everything to a certain purpose'.[12] The closer the Forms are to the highest Form, the more they may claim to be divine; therefore the heavenly spheres, the stars, the planets, are intelligent, eternal divine beings, imperishable even as individuals. In Aristotle's opinion the Olympic gods took their origin 'in a misconception of these ancient divine powers of nature'.[13]

d. *The Stoics*

The Stoics, like Plato and Aristotle, put forward a dualistic conception of the world. Gross matter, *ousia*, is in-formed by the spiritual, rational principle of *pneuma*, *aither* or fire, (the latter being to them an extremely subtle form of matter). The individual souls of animals, men and celestial bodies are parts of this universal world soul, so that all things are in sympathetic relations to each other, and all things are structured according to design. Nature as a whole is the world soul and intellect; it is identified with the Zeus of popular religion: 'of Jove all things are full', says Vergil.[14]

e. *Galen*

In the writings of the Greek physician Galen (*c.* 129–201), which exerted an enormous influence in subsequent ages, this same teleological concept, the same identification of God and nature, the same emphasis on the divine art, *techne*, are displayed. Because of this pious teleological concept Galen was, like Seneca, considered by the Christians of the Middle Ages and the Renaissance to have been basically a fellow-Christian. It is true that he provided the rare example of a pagan writer producing work in sympathy with the Mosaic story of creation, because he recognized a divine plan. However, he rejected the Mosaic account because the God of the Book of Genesis is completely free and not even restricted in his activities by the nature of matter.[15]

f. The Middle Ages

Greek theology and philosophy strongly influenced later Christian thought. The physical theology, or theological physics, of the Stoics combined with biblical conceptions when nature was considered as being entrusted with the care of the regular course of the world, in which the God of the Bible intervenes now and again. Medieval twelfth-century platonism (Bernard Silvestris, Alanus of Lille) placed nature as a kind of intermediate being between God and the world: 'Nature, by God's grace the vice-gerent and lieutenant of the kingdom of the world'.[16] The introduction of Aristotelian philosophy brought about another compromise between biblical theology and pagan philosophy. However, as we shall see below, there has been a never-ceasing protest from Christian theologians against this naturalism which detracted from God's sovereign power.

B. THE BIBLICAL VIEW

There is a radical contrast between the deification of nature in pagan religion and, in a rationalized form, in Greek philosophy, and the de-deification of nature in the Bible. By contrast with the nature-worship of its neighbours, the religion of Israel was a unique phenomenon. The God of

Israel, by his word, brings forth all things out of nothingness.[17] He is truly all-powerful: He was not opposed by any matter that had to be forced into order, and He did not have to reckon with eternal Forms; His sovereign will alone created and sustains the world. In the first chapter of Genesis it is made evident that absolutely nothing, except God, has any claim to divinity; even the sun and the moon, supreme gods of the neighbouring peoples, are set in their places between the herbs and the animals and are brought into the service of mankind.[18] The personal gods of the Greeks had an origin, in spite of their immortality. The God of the Bible is the only god who is immutable and eternal, unlike all created things which are liable to change and final destruction.[19] Nothing else has divine power, not even by delegation: 'The Lord is one; there is no one but He.'[20]

The New Testament proclaims again the message that there is no eternal cycle of nature or cycle of history. The history of the world moves towards its final destination and heaven and earth are destined to fall back into the nothingness from which they once emerged. Not only the creating, but also the upholding of the world belongs to God alone; that is to say, Jahveh is not a deistic supreme being who, after the creative act, leaves everything to the innate laws of nature, and He does not withdraw, like a platonic demiurge, into 'the way of being that belongs solely to Him'. He remains for ever the will and power behind all events[21]— Christ 'upholds all things by the word of His power'.[22] It is true that there is order in the living as well as in the non-living world[23]; but this is order existing not in its own right, but as a testimony to God's fatherly care for man and animals. The Bible knows nothing of 'Nature'[23a] but knows only 'creatures', who are absolutely dependent for their origin and existence on the will of God. Consequently, the natural world is admired as God's work and as evidence of its creator, but it is never adored. Nature can arouse in man a feeling of awe, but this is conquered by the knowledge that man is God's fellow-worker who shares with Him the rule of the fellow-creatures,[24] the 'dominion over the fish of the sea, and over the fowl of the air, and over the cattle, and over all the earth . . .'[25] Thus, in total contradiction to pagan religion, nature is not a deity to be feared and worshipped, but a work of God to be admired, studied and managed. When we compare pagan and biblical religions, we find a fundamental contrast between the ideas concerning God and man which have emerged. In the Bible God and nature are no longer both opposed to man, but God and man together confront nature. The denial that God coincides with nature implies the denial that nature is god-like.

C. FATHER, MAKER AND CREATOR OF THE WORLD

To most Greek philosophers nature was a living, divine organism, producing all things, all gods, men and animals, by generation. Hesiod thought that the earth generated the mountains, whereas according to the book of Genesis it was by God's command that the dry land was separated from the sea.

At first sight Plato's demiurge seems to be similar to the biblical creator. The demiurge kneads matter into the required forms, like a potter, while Saint Paul likewise compares the relation between God and man with that between the potter and the clay,[26] and the psalmist speaks of the work of God's fingers.[27] Yet, there are great differences. Firstly, in the Bible the image of the potter and the clay is only a metaphor expressing man's dependence, whereas with Plato the comparison goes deeper. The demiurge, like a human artificer making household utensils, has to bring together two existing things, the material and the plan, the one resisting the perfection of the work, the other restricting the freedom of its design. Secondly, Plato's demiurge leaves the sustaining of the universe to the world soul and he even delegates the construction of living beings, man included, to him, as this divine potter considers it beneath his dignity and beyond his power to make a mortal vessel. The creator in the Genesis account, on the other hand, considers his crowning act to be the creation of man. Thirdly, in the *Timaios* man is made by the secondary gods after the image of the universe—a mere image of the image of god; whereas in the Bible man is made after the image of God himself.

The concept of a world soul inevitably led to the idea that the *kosmos* is a living being and that generation is the fundamental act of nature. If the following of a rational design might have indicated that the demiurge was a maker, the organic character of the world showed rather that he was (perhaps in an allegorical sense) the father or begetter of the universe. Plato made him speak about 'the works whose maker and father I am'.[28] It was in fact this father-function which made it impossible for him to generate man immediately—like begets like. 'If I brought the mortals to life', he says, 'they would be equal to the gods'. The difference between a father and a maker is that a father transmits his own Form by self-reproduction (which does not imply that he commits a rational act), whereas a maker transmits a Form which has been contemplated by his Reason. These two images are united in Plato's *Timaios*.

In contradistinction to Plato, Aristotle did not use mythology. In his account of the becoming of things, nature herself possesses the properties both of a maker and a father. Like

Plato, Aristotle recognized two main aspects in nature: that she is *intelligible* and that she is a *living organism*. The first implied that nature makes things like an artificer, like a carpenter or a cook, though Aristotle would not go so far as to say that nature acts consciously or even less that she has any freedom. The products of nature are intelligible because they are the results of self-reproduction of rational Forms. That is, the idea of generation (begetting) of like by like was also stressed. The Form (*logos*) of the embryo is borrowed from the father who possessed it already.[29] That is, self-reproduction is a logical process, producing something intelligible, and it is a generative production of something similar that is also divine and alive. The fabrication and the generation thus represented the rational and the organistic aspect of the Greek vision of nature.

This statement is also true when applied to the concepts of the Stoics. According to Zeno, the soul (or fire) enters matter as a fertilizing sperm and thus brings life, order and law. The Stoics' term, 'rational seminal principles' (*logoi spermatikoi*), for the natures or essences of things, adequately and succinctly expresses the two aspects of the Greek conception of nature, that is, the notional, logical aspect of making things according to design, as well as the biological one of generating them. According to Cicero, it is necessary to look on nature as a rational being because she brings forth rational beings.[30] Moreover, nature should be regarded as comparable with a plant or an animal rather than with an inanimate body. The Latin term *natura-artifex* also implies the twin functions of begetter (procreator) and maker: *natura* is concerned with production from a seed, and *artifex* with the rational character of this process. But, again, this rational production was not a fabrication in a state of freedom; it remained within the bounds of an eternal biological repetition because the world was considered to be a living organism.

This great difference between the biblical concept of a transcendental creator evoking the world out of nothing by his free will, and the Greek concept of growth and generation by immanent divine nature, had far-reaching consequences. The further development of the science of nature was dependent to a significant degree upon which of these two concepts would emerge as its spiritual background. Scientific method rests on the preconceptions the scientist has about nature, and those preconceptions depend on, amongst other things, his belief about God. The Bible, however, does not offer a philosophical or scientific system. So it goes without saying that the Christian philosophers of late Antiquity and the Middle Ages, when taking over a science and philosophy which had a pagan religious background, met with great difficulties and found it hard to distinguish the wheat from the tares.

Now the idea of a divine creator implies the absolute dependence of the created things on him and also their total differentiation from him. The opinion prevailing amongst the Christian philosophers of the Midde Ages, however, was not wholly consistent with this conception. Nature was considered as a semi-independent power, and when things happened according to nature, this meant that they followed a pattern that seemed rational to the human mind, one which had been discovered by Aristotle. Nature, according to this scheme, accomplished the full being of her immanent Forms by means of efficient and final causes. In these latter, in a subtle way, the cosmic powers, the 'love' and the 'generation' of the old religion of nature, continued to play a role. In the Middle Ages, then, the biblical view was only superimposed on, and did not overcome, the Aristotelian conception. The regular order of nature was considered to be something instituted by God, but liable to be over-ruled by Him in a *super*-natural way (the term is significant) when performing a miracle. Thomas Aquinas considered one of the useful functions of natural philosophy to be to enable us to distinguish that which belongs only to God (for example miracles, or the origin of things) from that which belongs to nature. The Bible, however, attributes *all* events, however insignificant, immediately to God. Natural things are nothing but His instruments, and the order of nature is founded not on an immanent logic, but on God's care for his creatures. God does not intervene in an order of nature which is semi-independent; He acts either according to a regular pattern, or else in a more exceptional way, or even in a unique way.

D. THE MECHANISTIC WORLD PICTURE

Contrary perhaps to what one would have expected, a more fully biblical world view has, since the sixteenth century, favoured the rise of modern science and of the world picture connected with it. The model of the world as an organism was replaced by that of the world as a mechanism; the whole development from Copernicus to Newton has rightly been called the mechanization of the world picture.

Now it has often been said that the Greek atomists too had de-deified nature and that they, no less than the 'mechanical philosophers' of the seventeenth century, attributed all change to the union and disunion and the motion of small particles. And as, moreover, they did not share the opinion prevailing among the Greeks that 'all things are full of gods', they were, in this respect at least, closer to Christianity and modern science than Plato, Aristotle and the Stoics. From the standpoint of adherents of the ancient religion of nature, the Christians and the Epicureans alike were 'atheists'. In the same way in the seventeenth century the adherents of the old Aristotelian school considered that mechanical philosophy would necessarily lead to atheism; whereas, on the other hand, some of the Christian protagonists of the 'new philosophy' (Beeckman, Basso, Gassendi, Boyle) looked favourably upon the Epicureans. Boyle thought that the doctrine of 'matter and motion' gave more honour to God than the doctrine of 'nature' gave to Him, and that Aristotle did more damage to religion than did Epicurus.[31] At the same time he recognized that Epicurus and Lucretius set up, instead of the one God they rejected, an infinity of gods, the atoms, to which they attributed such divine properties as eternity and sovereignty. That is, he considered the difference between his and Epicurus's philosophy to be greater than the affinity. Here Boyle was right indeed, and not only from the religious but also from the scientific standpoint. Ancient atomism shared with mechanical philosophy the belief that change comes about through matter and motion, but atomism did not recognize design in nature. A mechanism, however, is a product of design. So the concept of the world as a machine not only excluded the organistic naturalism of Aristotle, but also the materialism of Epicurus. The image of a machine is connected with that of a maker apart from itself, that is with the theistic faith in a transcendent God. The man who compares the world with the clock of Strasburg, said Boyle, could accept a God as a creator and sustainer of it.[32]

The element of design in mechanistic philosophy does not arise from the 'natures' of things, but from the properties with which God endowed them. These properties may perhaps even lead to 'Forms' different from any manifested hitherto. Mechanistic philosophy also recognized final causes, but these were considered to belong to another level than that of pure physics—the end to which a clock had been made did not explain its behaviour. Teleology in mechanical philosophy is on a level higher than physical theory. Whereas a living organism suggests the idea of an immanent final cause (the maintenance of the life of the individual), a machine finds its reason for being in the plan of its maker and outside itself. A world organism has been *generated*; a world mechanism has been *fabricated*. That is why the latter fits in more suitably with a biblical view of the world.[33] So seventeenth century mechanistic philosophy was not a new compromise of Christianity, this time with ancient materialism instead of ancient organicism or idealism, but rather a step towards the Christianization and the emancipation of natural science. Neither the de-deification of the world by the materialists, nor the rationalization of the world by the idealists, has been able to find the right pattern for science. Evidently, the mechanization of the world picture (a radical de-deification in the biblical sense) was necessary to do this.

Of course, the machine model offers no adequate picture. The maker of a machine is under severe restrictions by the character of the materials, whereas the creator creates his materials himself; once it has been made, a machine has a certain independence, but the God of the biblical authors never abandons his work, as this would mean its reduction into nothingness. The image of a god-mechanician, then, is subordinate to that of a god-creator, but it is not at odds with it, as is the image of a god begetting the universe. Thus the idea of a world-machine, though not to be found in the Bible, fits in better with its spirit than the idea of a world-organism.

The Bible has a certain world view, that of the total dependence of the world on its Creator, but not a definite world picture. The picture of a world machine fits well with the idea of God as a maker. As, however, the activity of an omnipotent Creator has no human counterpart, the product of this activity, the whole world, cannot be adequately represented by any model. Nothing in nature can provide us with a real knowledge of God, for, as Francis Bacon said, 'All knowledge progresses by similarity; God is only similar to Himself and has nothing in common with any creature than by way of speech'.[34] What nature really is cannot be adequately expressed by the simile of a 'machine', and who God really is cannot be aptly represented by the term 'mechanician'. It cannot be done even by reducing natural science to mathematics and by calling God, 'for want of a wider word',[35] a great mathematician.

E. THE MECHANISTS' CRITIQUE OF THE ORGANISTIC WORLD VIEW

Some of the mechanistic philosophers and scientists of the seventeenth century, such as Basso, Boyle and Newton, strongly emphasized that neither the Forms of Aristotle nor the atoms of the moderns ought to be deified. They recognized the pagan element in much of the natural philosophy current in their time, and they considered the substantial Forms to be superfluous notions with harmful metaphysical connotations.

a. *Basso*

The French physician Sebastian Basso, writing in 1621,[36] rejected substantial Forms and Intelligences. In his opinion they were 'numina', the almost-divine powers which according to ancient Greek religion dwell in trees and springs. In the current scholastic philosophy it was held that they acted as God's lieutenants. Basso, on the other hand, was of the opinion that God's 'intellect' works in all things, moves them and leaves them to their final purpose, so that special 'natures' or Forms are superfluous. There is, in his opinion, only one general 'nature', one general cause, namely God Himself. Everything that was formerly attributed to nature, Basso ascribed immediately to God: 'He, who is present everywhere, works all things immediately', as Scripture teaches us. Basso condemned—because it created more confusion—the opinion put forward by the Jesuits that there is a co-operation of the innate nature of things with God. In his opinion nothing should diminish God's absolute power and sovereignty. The sustaining of the world is a continual process, so that the concept of nature, as a vice-gerent of God is wholly superfluous. As, however, God acts according to order and rule, it may *seem* as if the various species aspire to their own end by some innate power, which could be called 'nature'. Basso, then, maintained teleology on the religious or metaphysical level, but on the level of physics he did not hesitate to say that atoms move by chance and not according to a final aim. That is, Basso, in contrast to the ancient atomists, discarded final causes from a methodological, but not from an ontological, point of view.

b. *Boyle*

This de-deification of nature and natural science on biblical grounds was propounded even more clearly by Robert Boyle in 1666 and 1682. In his critical examination of the concept of nature[37] he maintains that nature, usually presented as an almost divine being, is but a 'notional thing'. The 'vulgarly received notion' is an insult to God and an impediment to a reliable investigation of His works. God, as a skilful engineer, has put the laws of motion into matter, and He maintains them by His continual co-operation, for which He does not require a 'lieutenant or vice-gerent'. 'Nature' is not a 'separate agent' but a 'system of rules'. Boyle preferred the term 'rule' to that of 'law of nature', because a law is a rule of action dictated by a higher will; evidently only persons endowed with reason would be able to receive 'laws'. The Platonic 'world soul' is, in Boyle's opinion, of the same kind as the Aristotelian 'nature'. He thoroughly disliked the then popular expression 'God and nature do nothing in vain', as these two are mentioned together 'not as creator and creature, but as two conjoined governors, in the manner of the two Roman consuls'. As against the necessity of Nature, Boyle maintained that God is 'a most free agent', who did not create the world of necessity, and who constituted it when there was no substance besides Himself, and no creature to which He owed any obligation or by which He could be restricted. Evidently Boyle did not regard Plato as an 'Attic Moses'!

The notion of Nature outlived the 'vulgar philosophy', that is, the scholasticism of Boyle's time. In the nineteenth century Darwin spoke about natural selection in the same anthropomorphic way, saying, for example, 'Natural Selection picks out with unerring skill the best varieties', so that the geologist Charles Lyell felt obliged to ask him whether he was not deifying natural selection too much. Even today a reference to Nature serves as the invocation of a deity for many members of the church scientific, while an appeal to what is 'natural' still seems to have the force of divine command for some leading members of the church catholic. Deification of nature is still alive, and the fact that this deity has no special cult does not prove anything to the contrary. There was no special cult of Nature in Antiquity, and no temples were erected to it, yet it was adored under the names of other gods.

It must be admitted that something of the old notion of nature remained in the mechanistic philosophy of Boyle, as in that of Newton. Boyle declared that when matter and motion are not sufficient to explain phenomena, this is an indication of God's miraculous intervention.[37b] A similar semi-deistic vestige is to be found with Newton, who believed that God now and again readjusts the world machine. Yet Newton gave a clear verdict on the relation between God and His creatures, when he rejected the idea that God, omnipresent in the world, would consequently be the soul of the world: 'He is not the soul of the world, but Lord over all . . . For God is a word expressing a relation, and it refers to servants . . . a Being, however perfect, without rule, cannot be called Lord God, for we say my God, your God, the God of Israel . . . but not my Eternal, your Eternal, the Eternal of Israel . . . or my Infinite, or my Perfect; these are titles that bear no relation to servants . . . for a God without rule, providence and design, is nothing but Necessity and Nature. . . .'[38] It is true that Newton also believed that the common course of nature was the effect of God's immediate sustaining activity. In practice, however, the mechanicism of many followers of Boyle and Newton showed a tendency to a semi-deism which perhaps differed in degree but not in essence from that of the adherents of 'vulgar philosophy'.

F. THE RADICAL CRITIQUE OF NATURALISM

Final causes or 'natures' might have been discarded as semi-independent causes of natural events, but the efficient causes remained, and they too implied a kind of independence of the material world in relation to God. The radical critique of these last vestiges of ancient naturalism came from Malebranche and Berkeley, who freed the physical notion of force from its hidden metaphysical character.

a. *Malebranche*

The late Michael B. Foster has pointed out that, as the cosmogony of Hesiod was reflected in the philosophy of Aristotle, so the doctrine of creation of the Book of Genesis found its counterpart in the philosophical critique by Berkeley and Hume of the idea of immanent forces in things, which, as 'causes', produced 'effects'. Even before Berkeley, however, the Oratorian priest Nicole Malebranche (1638–1715) had already put forward a similar critique. He pointed out that vulgar philosophy (scholasticism) had mixed up Christian religion with pagan philosophy when considering substantial Forms as true causes. If, however, something is said to work by its own nature (however subordinate to the supreme Cause), it assumes the character of a deity (however much subordinate to the highest God). Thus, reverence for pagan philosophy led to the unconscious acceptance of pagan ideas; 'the heart may be Christian, but the mind is pagan at the bottom'. As there is only one God, there can be only one Cause—'the nature of each thing is nothing but the will of God'.[39]

Malebranche's critique, however, touched also on efficient causes. For instance, when two balls collide, the one is not the 'cause' of the motion of the other—and the collision is only the occasion on which the author of nature acts in such and such a way. Malebranche pointed out that 'God cannot make his creatures into true causes, He cannot make them gods', and he said that Forms and Powers are

'the little gods of the heathen', introduced by the Evil One
to occupy the hearts which the Creator has made to belong
to Himself. It is a manifestation of the philosophy of the
Serpent; since the Fall the human mind has been wholly
pagan. The adherents of this doctrine worship the fictions
of their own minds, in the same way as the heathen adore
the works of their own hands. Mechanistic philosophy, on
the other hand, which is held up as a scarecrow to weak
minds, recognizes the one Cause only, and shows that all
secondary causes (or the gods of philosophy) are nothing but
powerless matter.[40] When one of the participants in Malebranche's *Dialogue on Metaphysics*[41] chides the other because
he refers too much to the truths of faith, the answer is that
without these truths there are thousands of difficulties to
which he would not find an answer, including for example
the question as to whether things outside the mind really
exist. Here the authority of faith teaches that God created
the world and that this changes all phenomena into realities.

Malebranche recognized that mechanistic philosophy
could fall easily into the error of believing that, once God
had created the world, the world then existed in its own right.
In his opinion, however, this would amount to independence, and he preferred to think that, as soon as God stops
willing the world to exist, it will cease to exist; the sustaining of the creatures is a 'continued creation'. Here Malebranche clearly saw the difference between the notion of
creator and that of maker. In his opinion it was wrong to
think about God and his works by analogy with human
activities. The architect, he stated, has to deal with already
existing materials and the house he builds with them will
continue its existence after his death.[42] The universe, on the
other hand, has been brought forth from nothing, and
it so completely depends on God that it would be re-

duced to nothing if God ceased to maintain it by His will.[43]

b. *Berkeley*

The critique of the Anglican bishop George Berkeley (1685–1753) was perhaps even more stringent. He had to purge science of the deistic tendencies which arose in scientific circles after Newton, as Malebranche had fought against those which sprang from the philosophy of Descartes. Berkeley repudiated the tendency to transfer anthropomorphic notions, such as will, cause or force, to material things. On the other hand, because man had been created after the image of God, he was authorized to transfer, by a magnifying process, certain human properties, such as will, to God[44]. That is, Berkeley saw that the fact of man's being-an-image-of-God lay primarily in his having a will rather than in his 'mechanical' capacities. For Berkeley, physics had a purely descriptive character. Although he accepted the mechanistic world picture, Berkeley denied that there could be any efficacy in the form, size, motion, or forces of the particles. He thought that even Newton had not been radical enough in his rejection of independent entities (natures), saying that Newton's absolute space and absolute motion and forces were 'children of imagination' and 'phantoms'.[45] In particular the idea of the existence of matter was annoying to Berkeley. In his opinion, these notions were beyond experience and ought not to be admitted into scientific philosophy. No thing whatever has any activity in itself, and even the impressions things make upon our minds are the results of acts of will of God; even the existence of things is only in the mind of God: 'so long as they are not perceived by any created spirit, they must . . . subsist in the mind of some eternal spirit'.[46]

Berkeley rejected the concept of 'nature' for a methodological reason—it is an empty word—and for a religious reason—it is used by pagans and philosophers who ascribe things to Nature, to Matter and Fate, whereas Holy Scripture attributes them immediately to the hand of God. Berkeley, like Malebranche recognized that his conception was equivalent to 'continual creation', and, like Newton, he emphasized that God is concerned with our smallest thoughts and actions.

In his treatise *On Motion* (1721), Berkeley thoroughly criticizes the principles of mechanical philosophy, saying that such symbols as force, weight, attraction might be useful for calculations, but that they do not reveal the nature of motion. Science (experience) does not prove their existence, as its only task is to reduce the multitude of phenomena to general rules, connecting what precedes with what follows. Science indicates the relations between phenomena by using symbols, like 'force'. These, however, should not be regarded as real causes, as it is impossible to distinguish the activity of a body from its motions.[47]

About one hundred and fifty years afterwards, in 1882, the English physicist J. B. Stallo put forward a similar critique of the notion of force,[48] and Clerk Maxwell took the same line. The only reality of the notion of force, according to Stallo, is that it connects all physical phenomena with each other. A recent author put the same idea in other words, saying that there was no room for the notion of force, in its metaphysical sense of causal activity, in the science of the empirically measurable.[49]

Berkeley, of course, recognized that there is order in the world, but like other Christian philosophers before him, he attributed these so-called laws of nature not to inner necessity but to the exercise of the free will of God, who thereby makes life possible. The bishop here took his place in a long line of tradition, between Saint Augustine who said that the 'will of God is the necessity of things' and Charles Kingsley (1860) who said that what we call laws of nature 'are not really Laws of Nature, but merely customs of God'. God could have made any one phenomenon the announcement of the next, and therefore Berkeley emphasized that only empirical research could give certainty about these rules and that all logical deductions had to give way to such research. His radical supranaturalism thus led to a strictly mathematically-descriptive empiricism. Berkeley believed that nothing works by itself, that only God works; nothing exists in itself, but it exists only in God; there is no absolute space and time; there are no efficient causes and forces, and there is no existence at all apart from God.

Berkeley's subtle and abstract idealism converges in the simplicity of its conclusions with the naive realism of those who sit down before fact like little children. He was willing to agree with those who maintain that what we perceive does really exist, but he repudiated those who appealed to the testimony of the senses for the demonstration of things like matter or substance, which he considered to be philosophical fictions. He said that it was not he himself who was sceptical about physical reality, but those who degraded the visible world for the benefit of a pretended reality behind it.[50] That is, the world of phenomena was more real to him than that of the Forms, Natures and Ideas of ancient and medieval philosophy, and also more real than the world of the atoms and forces of mechanistic Newtonian science (or, one might add, than that of the electrons, fields, *psi-*functions and so forth, of modern science). In general such things are considered to be more 'real', more 'true' in physics than the phenomena immediately perceived. Berkeley, however, considered them to be convenient

fictions, put forward in order to interconnect those phenomena so that we can manipulate and classify natural things.[50]

c. *Retrospect*

We have reviewed different conceptions of the relation of
God to the world: that of the father to the child, that of the
artificer to the artificial product, that of the creator to the
creatures. The first-mentioned led to the consideration of
the world as a divine and organic being, which possessed an
intelligible character. This found its counterpart in the
science of Plato and Aristotle, and of most of the scholastic
and Renaissance philosophers. The second favoured the
image of the world as a machine; and led to a mechanistic
world picture as delineated by Descartes, Gassendi, Boyle,
Huygens and Newton. It is quite remarkable that as early a
mechanistic writer as Basso should already have recognized
the substantial Forms, so firmly entrenched in religious
orthodoxy, as pagan 'numina' in disguise, and that scientists
and philosophers of backgrounds as widely different as those
of Boyle, Malebranche and Berkeley agreed in making it
even more evident that the Forms were the idols of a widespread superstition. No less remarkable was Malebranche's
and Berkeley's insight that the atoms, forces and causes of
the New Philosophy—though more useful in building a
scientific system—were also unduly deified fictions of the
human mind.

The mechanistic world picture was then adapted (albeit
with some reserve and stressing its inadequacies) to the conception of God as a creator. This adaptation thus led to a
positive and empiricist conception of science which was
accepted by such men as Pascal and Berkeley, and to a large
extent also by Boyle and Newton. It formed the basis of
that rational empiricism which has become the legitimate

method of modern science. The scientist of today, when using mechanical or other pictures or models, considers them as means of rational description and not as explications of the essence of the world. The world of the physicist is a translation of the world of phenomena into symbols that are more liable to mathematical manipulation and whose consequences may be easily translated back into external phenomena. This has been clearly recognized during the last century by many outstanding physicists from Hertz to Heisenberg.[51] Most scientists of the nineteenth and twentieth centuries, when taking this view, may have been unconscious of the fact that the metaphysical foundations of their discipline stemmed, in spite of all secularization, in great part from the biblical concept of God and creation.

NOTES TO CHAPTER I

1. O. Gilbert, *Die meteorologischen Theorien des griechischen Altertums*, Leipzig, 1907, p. 70.
2. Aristotle, *Metaphysics*, i. 3.
3. W. Jaeger, *Die Theologie der frühen griechischen Denker*, Stuttgart, 1953, p. 87.
4. Empedocles, B 21, 23. The Pre-Socratics are cited after: H. Diels, *Fragmente der Vorsokratiker*, 5th ed.
5. F. M. Cornford, *From Religion to Philosophy*, London, 1912, pp. 12, 13, 16, 118, 119.
6. Herakleitos, B 94.
7. O. Gilbert in: Arch. f. Gesch. Phil., xxii, p. 279.
8. Cf. Plato, *Timaios*, 30 E.
9. Plato, *Republic*, 136 C.
10. Plato, *Timaios*, 28 C.
11. Plato, *Phaidros*, 246 D.
12. Aristotle, *De part. animal.*, i. 1, 641 b.
13. Aristotle, *Metaph.*, xii. 8, 1074 b.
14. Vergil, *Bucol.*, iii. 60.
15. Galen, *De usu partium*, xi. 14.

16. Cf. E. R. Curtius, *Europäische Literatur und lateinisches Mittelalter*, Bern, 1954², Kap. VI.
17. Psalms 33:9.
18. Genesis I:17; Psalms 104:19.
19. Hebrews 1:10–12; Psalms 102:26–28.
20. Isaiah 45:5.
21. Psalms 135:6–7, 9–10.
22. Hebrews 1:3.
23a. Here and elsewhere, 'Nature' (with capital N) is used to indicate the deification or personification of nature.
23. Psalms 104:19, 27.
24. Psalms 8:4–17.
25. Genesis 1:26.
26. Romans 9:20–21.
27. Psalms 8:4.
28. Plato, *Timaios*, 41 A; 37 C; 28 C.
29. Aristotle, *De gen. anim.*, i, 734 b.
30. Cicero, *De natura deorum*, ii. 34.
31. Boyle, *A Free Inquiry into the Vulgarly Received Notion of Nature*, Sect. I.
32. Boyle, *A Free Inquiry*, Sect. I.
33. M. B. Foster in: *Mind*, 44 (1935), pp. 439–466.
34. F. Bacon, *Valerius Terminus*, c. 1.
35. James Jeans, *The Mysterious Universe*, Cambridge, 1930, pp. 134, 136.
36. Seb. Basso, *Philosophiae naturalis adversus Aristotelem libri XII*, Amsterodami, 1649 (sec. ed.).
37. Boyle, *A Free Inquiry into the Vulgarly Received Notion of Nature* (1682).
37b. See above, p. 13.
38. Isaac Newton, *Philosophiae Naturalis Principia Mathematica*. Sec. ed., London, 1713. Scholium generale.
39. N. Malebranche, *De la recherche de la vérité*, VI, 2, c. 3.
40. N. Malebranche, *De la recherche de la vérité*. Of course Malebranche here presents 'mechanistic' philosophy in his own, purified, version.
41. Malebranche, *Entretiens sur la métaphysique*, ix. 5.
42. Cf. below Descartes, Ch. II, p. 42.
43. Malebranche, *Entretiens*, vii. 8.
44. G. Berkeley, *Three Dialogues between Hylas and Philonous*, III.
45. Berkeley, *Siris* 249, 292, 293.
46. Berkeley, *The Principles of Human Knowledge*, 6.
47. Berkeley, *De motu*, 11.
48. J. B. Stallo, *The Concepts and Theories of Modern Physics*, London, 1882, pp. 166–167.
49. M. Jammer, *The Concepts of Force*, 1957, p. 229.
50. Berkeley, *Three Dialogues*, III.

51. 'Science is not a philosophy developing a world-view of nature as a whole or about the essence of things' (W. Heisenberg, *The Physicist's Conception of Nature*, London, 1958, p. 152).

    Heinrich Hertz, *Prinzipien der Mechanik* (1876), Einleitung. *Gesammelte Werke*, III, Leipzig, 1894.

CHAPTER II

REASON AND EXPERIENCE

A. RATIONALISM AND EMPIRICISM IN ANTIQUITY AND THE MIDDLE AGES

a. *Rationalism and Empiricism*

Science works upwards from phenomena to a rational system of relations, explanations and predictions, and ends again in testing these by experiments made in the world of phenomena from which it started. When the rational element gets more than its due, it becomes rationalism, which considers rationality to be the criterion for reality and allots a secondary role to observation and experimentation. A rational empiricism, on the other hand, recognizes that reason is indispensable for the creation of order, but that it has to submit to what has been given in the world; it has an open eye for the contingency of the existence and the way of being of things.

According to the Greek idealistic philosophers nature is full of reason and logical necessity, to which even Plato's demiurge had to submit. The God of the Bible, however, Jahveh, is a God who needed to obey nothing, not even the Ideas. Between these two views there is so fundamental an opposition in their concept of the world that this opposition influences the method of acquiring scientific knowledge about the universe. The logical Necessity which reigns over a world of eternal self-regenerating Forms implies a science obeying the dictates of reason; the biblical conception of a world fabricated and created by a free act of will of God implies a science subject to data and facta, things given and made, whether they are rational or not. All efforts to reconcile Athens and Jerusalem on this point led to inner tensions and new controversies. One of the crucial questions at issue was that which asked whether things were good because God willed them, or whether God willed them because they were good. Voluntarism stood over against intellectualism. Could God do anything He wanted to do, or was He restricted by the nature of things?

The choice between a rationalistic and an empirical scientific method was largely determined by this and other theological considerations. If God is the father of nature (or if He is identified with her), and if, moreover, generation is a logical process, then man—being a part and a son of the logos that penetrates the universe—should have an intuitive knowledge of nature. If, however, God is a creator not bound to any model or final purpose, then man can only find out *a posteriori* how far the data of nature are comprehensible to human reason.

Now the Bible proclaims again and again that the thoughts of God are not those of man.[1] God does not work according to human expectations and His ways, in revealing Himself in Jesus of Nazareth, are 'a foolishness to the heathen'.[2] The apostles proclaimed, not those things which seemed reasonable to them, but those things which they 'had seen with their eyes and their hands had handled'.[3] This, transferred to the field of science, means that just as the faith of the Christians was founded not on a cleverly excogitated system, but on what they had recognized to be hard facts, so science has to accept facts, even when they seem to be against reason and rule.

b. *The Rationalism of the Greek Philosophers*

Greek science on the other hand bore a strongly rationalistic character which is particularly evident in its attitude towards change. Change is incomprehensible to the human mind because a real change is like a new creation; a thing becomes that which it was not before. Therefore the Eleatic philosophers denied the reality of any change. For this same reason Plato considered mathematics one of the best examples of true science, as it deals with things which are not liable to change, whereas physics is much less certain, as it deals with things that are liable to change. Therefore, the phenomena visible in the heavens do not correspond to true, real astronomy for the same reason that the triangle drawn in the sand is not the same as the true subject of geometry, the ideal triangle. A science founded on observation could not be a true science. Consequently, Plato laughs at the Pythagoreans who make the same mistake as the astronomers, for while the latter turn their eyes to visible things to learn true astronomy, the former give their ears to audible sounds to learn harmonics. Even Aristotle, in spite of considering change to be intelligible[4] and in spite of his admission that all knowledge begins through the senses, developed a physical system largely by deductive reasoning.

c. *Scholastic Rationalism and its Medieval Critics*

Aristotle had established *a priori* that the heavens must have an eternal circular motion, that the earth must exist, and that there must be four elements. Everything in his universe is connected with all other things by a law of logical necessity.

Many medieval philosophers[5a], in particular the Averroists, believed that, when creating the universe, God had to follow this law. Consequently, He could not make matter without the help of the heavenly bodies, which stood between Him and the earth. The fundamental idea was that there could not be any innovation in effects, as there could not be any change in the supreme cause (God). The existence of God was thus connected in this reasoning with a long chain of natural events, from the heavenly motions down to the most trivial terrestrial phenomena. Thus the philosophers came to the thesis that: 'if the heavens would stand still, fire would not burn tow, because God would not exist'.

In reaction to these conceptions the bishop of Paris, Étienne Tempier, at the instigation of Pope John XXI in 1277 condemned 219 theses, many of which propounded this necessitarianism which restricted God's power by the dictate of what seemed reasonable to Man. Of course, what really mattered to Tempier was only the full recognition of the sovereignty and freedom of God, but in rejecting any limits to these, he unintentionally took away limitations to scientific theorizing as well. Not only the theology of necessity was at stake, but also the natural science of necessity. Among the theses he condemned were those that suggested that God could not make an empty space; that He could not create new species; that He could not make more than one planetary system, and that He could not give other than circular motions to the heavenly bodies. All these prohibitions hampered the freedom of scientific research; all of them in the long run turned out to be false.

d. *Nominalist Empiricism*

A hundred years afterwards the nominalists revived this voluntaristic theology and demonstrated in a more explicit way its relevance to Science. The nominalists rejected deductions from the nature of things; substantial Forms were to them but names, *nomina*; they found the only full reality in individual things. In principle, this implied a stronger emphasis on empirical facts as the basis of science, and thus a more empirical approach. They placed their confidence in critical reason, not in theoretical reason.

Jean Buridan (*c.* 1350) maintained that God 'in his most free will' might have created things that were not conformable to our reasonable, 'natural', expectations. God could have created a different world order and this would then also have been 'natural'. In his opinion, there is no simply necessary subjection to efficient causes except to God Himself. Perhaps God is the only efficient cause, and fire would burn wood even if there were no celestial bodies.[5b] Only the relation between the phenomena and *God* is necessary; all other relations are not. That is, the contingency of nature was as fully recognized by Buridan in the fourteenth century as it would be by Berkeley in the eighteenth century.

Nicole Oresme (1377) who belonged to the same school, rejected the thesis that there could not be a void. He argued that our understanding depends on the senses and these, being material, cannot yield an adequate notion of the immaterial. A void outside the world transcends our comprehension; the same would be the case with a rectilinear movement of the heavens. But the thesis that this would be impossible was condemned in Paris: 'It depends on the will of God', who moves the heavens as it pleases Him. Oresme rejected the thesis that tow would not burn if the heavens stood still, referring again to the Paris condemnation.[6] In his opinion Aristotle's reasoning could not prove that the heavens move in circles and that the earth stands still, for it depends on God's will, and for Him there is no necessity whatever to cause those motions. In the same way, another nominalist, Heinrich von Langenstein, believed that many new species would arise in the course of time. Evidently, he did not believe that God's creative activity is bound to a pre-existent limited store of eternal Forms.

Of course, there was some risk of credulity being allowed full rein so as to admit, by an appeal to God's omnipotence, the possibility of existence of anything imaginable, however fantastic it might be. Therefore Thomas Aquinas' rationalistic and naturalistic tendencies are sometimes praised by modern critics as being more 'scientific' than the 'theological' view supported by the nominalists. But whereas in Thomism incomprehensible things were considered supernatural and miraculous,[7] the nominalists were prone to consider them natural. It should be emphasized that what matters is not what the logical consequences of a certain attitude are thought to be but what those consequences were in historical reality.

It turns out, then, that in fact the nominalists were less inclined to miracle-mongering than any other medieval thinkers. In their conception God was a God of order. Thus Oresme thought that credulity was the source of many allegedly non-natural events. It brought destruction to science and great danger to religion; many cases of witchcraft might be attributed to self-suggestion and extortion of confessions. On the other hand, Oresme pointed out that many natural events, like, for instance, the fall of a stone, or the phenomena of combustion, are as incomprehensible to reason as the resurrection of the body. Therefore Oresme concluded with the Socratic verdict: 'Truly, rightly considered, these things are less known than some articles of faith. Therefore, this alone I know with certainty, that I do not know anything with certainty.'

It was precisely the fact that the nominalists expected only probabilities rather than absolute certainties in science, which allowed them to build their scientific system with greater freedom. Their principle of economy—no more causes should be admitted than strictly necessary—implied

34

a simplification of the scientific system.[8] In recognizing the fact that we do not arrive at a thorough understanding, but at best at an exact description of nature, Oresme anticipated not only Pascal and Boyle, but also some of the great scientists of the twentieth century.

B. EMPIRICISM AND RATIONALISM IN THE BEGINNING OF THE SEVENTEENTH CENTURY

a. *Mathematical Empiricism of Galileo and Kepler*

Kepler and Galileo, two of the founders of modern science, believed with Plato that God worked according to mathematical models when creating the world. There was, however, an essential difference between their standpoint and that of the great Greek philosopher. Plato believed that matter was an impediment to the exact mirroring of mathematical Ideas in the world of phenomena (the mathematical laws of astronomy and acoustics are not fully expressed in that world). Kepler and Galileo, on the other hand, believed that the Creator fully realized His mathematical plan in the universe. Matter seemed to them to be no hindrance to God's creative activity; 'where matter is, there is geometry', says Kepler,[9] and Galileo was of the same opinion. Moreover, to them experience was not irrelevant. In their opinion, the mathematical Forms are in the mind, but only experience can decide which of them have been imprinted on the material world. Thus Kepler and Galileo, in contrast to Plato, put forward a mathematical empiricism.

This was quite evident in one of the most decisive moments in the history of science. It had been a dogma of the 'church scientific', up to the time of Kepler, that movements in the heavens could be nothing but uniform and circular. Everywhere, everybody had always held this to be true *a priori*;

Platonists and Aristotelians, Idealists and Nominalists, Copernicus and Galileo had accepted this dogma and Kepler himself was thoroughly convinced of its truth. Yet a difference of eight minutes between observation and calculation of the orbit of the planet Mars forced him, after a struggle of several years, to abandon this dogma of circularity and to postulate a non-uniform motion in elliptical orbits. He submitted to given facts rather than maintaining an age-old prejudice; in his mind a Christian empiricism gained the victory over platonic rationalism; a lonely man submitted to facts and broke away from a tradition of two thousand years. With full justice he could declare: 'These eight minutes paved the way for the reformation of the whole of astronomy', and it was with full justice, too, that in 1609 he gave to his book the title *New Astronomy*. In spite of his great respect for the 'divine philosopher' Kepler criticized the master; for Plato did not recognize that the perfection and necessity of the mathematical Forms took their origin in God's will, but instead founded them, without God, in the mathematical Ideas themselves and thus 'violated piety in some way'.

b. *Natural-historical Empiricism*

Even before Kepler and Galileo appeared on the scene, the certainty of the traditional and rather rationalistic world picture suffered some severe shocks as a result of discoveries in natural history not connected with any revolutionary theory. The ancients had rationally demonstrated that the tropical regions were uninhabitable because of the scorching heat. Towards the end of the fifteenth century, however, the Portuguese navigators passed the equator and found that the tropics and also the southern hemisphere were inhabited. In particular the fact that those discoveries were made by mariners, engineers, artificers, pilots, that is, by 'uneducated' people, gave a blow to the reputation of scholarly speculations in natural philosophy.[9b] The sixteenth century Portuguese poet Camoens wrote: 'I have seen things of which the uneducated mariners, who have only long experience as their teacher, proclaim the truth—whereas the scholars, who judge by science and pure reason only, demonstrate that they are not true or are misunderstood'. Sixty years later the English clergyman William Watts (1633) put it even more bluntly when he said: 'The thoughts of the philosophers have been contradicted by the unexpected observations of the navigators'.

Similar things happened in astronomy. Aristotle and his followers had demonstrated that no change could ever occur in the heavens. In 1572, however, a new star arose in Cassiopeia, visible to everybody. It was explained by some as a sublunar phenomenon, but Tycho Brahe proved that it must be above the moon. He saw the star for the first time when going from his laboratory to his observatory. As he could not believe his eyes, he asked his assistants whether they saw it too. Even then they did not feel sure and they only believed what they saw when some peasants confirmed it. Tycho remarked that it was mainly unlearned people and not astronomers who reported the new phenomenon.[10] Evidently, in general, the learned only saw what they believed to be possible.

Later on, another Aristotelian dogma, that of the impossibility of empty space, crumbled before facts. In this connection Pascal scornfully said that simple workmen had been able to convince of error those great men that are called 'philosophers'.[11] It was, then, these unlearned men who witnessed to the unexpected events which seemed impossible to the learned, who were the most ready to believe 'what they saw with their eyes and touched with their hands'. This expression was often used in the many 'histories' of observations and experiments written by semi-'educated' artificers. The Huguenot potter Bernard Palissy, for example, promised his visitors to teach them more within two hours by touching and seeing fossils than they could learn by fifty years' study from the books of the philosophers.[12]

Empirical demonstration now became more convincing than rational proof. Reason had to adapt itself to Experience, now that 'New Philosophy called all in doubt' (Donne). And reason did adapt itself. An early example is D. João de Castro, who remarked that the inhabitability of the tropical zone once seemed to be against Reason, but men have seen that it is inhabited, and now 'it seems the most reasonable thing in the world'.[13] To consider something 'rational' often amounts to being accustomed to it, as was clearly recognized by John Donne in an Easter sermon: 'There is nothing that God has established in the constant course of nature, and which therefore is done everyday, but would seem a Miracle and exercise our admiration if it were done but once . . . and only the daily doing takes off the admiration'. But an acquiescence in the seemingly absurd often occurred even before familiarity had taken the sting out of it. For instance, the Netherlands scientist Isaac Beeckman (1588–1637), one of the early defenders of the atomistic philosophy, concluded that this system contained an antinomy which nobody, himself included, could explain away: the atoms should be perfectly hard as well as perfectly elastic. Nevertheless, he decided to stick to atomism, because he thought it to be the best theory available.[14]

Such cases prove that the humbling experience of the

discoveries had made many scientists ready to give up the pretension to a wholly rational explanation of the world and to content themselves with a more or less mathematical description, revealing, if possible, causal relations between the phenomena. Similar situations arose again and again, This has happened in our own time, for example when Bohr made the seemingly absurd supposition that electrons move in their orbits without loss of energy; or again when physicists represented electrons by different models, sometimes conceived as particles, sometimes as waves.

c. *Francis Bacon's Natural-Historical Empiricism*

In the beginning of the seventeenth century Francis Bacon became the advocate of the new natural-historical empiricism. Though he hardly contributed anything to science proper, he exerted a wide influence on the scientists. He was perfectly conscious of the semi-pagan character of the old science. Therefore, in spite of his aversion to using the Bible as a kind of scientific textbook, it remains true that his attitude, as Professor B. Farrington says, might be summarized in the slogan: 'Out with Aristotle and in with the Bible'. In Bacon's opinion the root of all evil in science is the violation of the truth of nature by rationalistic prejudice. 'We copy the sin of our first parents. . . . They wished to be like God, but their posterity wish to be even greater. For we create worlds, we direct and domineer over Nature, we will have it that all things are as in our folly we think they should be, not as it seems fittest to the divine wisdom, or as they are found to be in fact . . . we clearly impress the stamp of our own image on the creatures and the works of God, instead of carefully examining and recognising in them the stamp of the creator himself.' Thus we lost our dominion over nature, 'because we desire to be like God and to follow the dictates of our own reason'. And then Bacon implores his readers in almost biblical language to 'discard these preposterous philosophies which have . . . led experience captive, and triumphed over the works of God; and to approach with humility and veneration to unroll the volume of creation'. Again and again Bacon criticized the intellectualism of the Greeks, their neglect of experiments and their premature construction of theories on a too narrow basis of facts. Only contact with the reality of the world of phenomena would, in Bacon's opinion, force our minds into soberness and modesty: 'When the mind of man works upon nature, the creatures of God, it is limited thereby, but if it works upon itself or upon a too small part of material things, it spins out laborious webs of learning.' That is, the restoration of science required first of all the collecting of more facts, a so-called natural history. Only after that would it be time to start theorizing afresh.

The analogy between the two books (Scripture and Nature) irresistibly presented itself here. Christian religion claimed to be based on 'historical' (real) phenomena, observed by the believer or known from reliable witnesses. Science, the interpretation of the book of creatures, is also founded on phenomena. Bacon thought that man could never search too far either in the book of God's word or in the book of God's works, in divinity or in science. As the School philosophers, in his opinion, had proudly substituted their own inventions for 'the oracle of God's word', 'so, in the inquisition of nature, they even left the oracle of God's works' and adored the deformed images of their own minds or a few received authors. Bacon even held that Christ, when saying 'You err, not knowing the Scriptures, nor the power of God', was referring to the two books, the Scriptures and the creatures.[14a]

C. CARTESIANISM

a. *Descartes' Theological Voluntarism*

It is strange that the triumph of rational empiricism was so soon followed by the rise of Cartesian rationalism. Voluntarism in theology was related to empiricism in science,[15] whereas intellectualism in theology was often connected with rationalism in science.[16] In spite of Descartes' scientific rationalism, however, his theological conceptions bore a decidedly voluntaristic character. Man was made after God's image, but, in Descartes' opinion, this does not imply so great a similarity that man should be able to find out God's design in nature. Even freedom of will in man is quite different from that in God; man can not find what is good, for this has already been done by the Creator. 'The Idea of Good did not force God to choose one thing above another.' The reason why all things, according to the Book of Genesis, were good 'is that He willed to make them as they are'.[17] Even the eternal truths, which to us seem absolutely incontrovertible, need not be so to God: 'The mathematical verities are as much fixed by God and depend as much on Him, as all the other creatures; he who says that they are independent of Him, makes Him into a Jupiter or Saturn and submits Him to Fate and Necessity'. We might say that 'God can do everything we understand, but we may not say that He cannot do what we do not understand, for it would be presumptuous to think that our imagination reaches as far as His power'. If He had willed it to be so, the three angles of the triangle would not have been equal to two right angles; these truths are no more necessarily linked up with His essence than with any other 'creature'.

The God of Descartes is not the Father of the universe ('the eternal truths do not emanate from God like the rays from the sun') and He is more than its maker. God is the absolutely sovereign creator, who suffers no independent nature beside Himself, either as Ideas, or as matter: 'the Architect is the cause of the house, and the father of the son, as to his coming-to-be, but the work can continue to exist without the cause . . . but God is the cause of created things, not only as to their coming-to-be but also as to their being'.[18] In Descartes' metaphysics, then, all conditions for the development of a positive science seem to be fulfilled. His belief that all things were just given could have been a powerful stimulus to an empiristic methodology; his stress on God's inscrutable and incomprehensible will could have blocked the way to rationalism.

b. *Descartes' Rationalism in Science*

In fact, however, Descartes did not turn out to be one of the founders of rational empiricism, but produced rather a deductive, rationalistic cosmological system. What, then, was the reason for this paradoxical situation? The reason is that in Descartes' opinion, God gave us minds of such a sort that we must recognize as rational and possible in nature that which it pleased God to put into nature, and that if we immediately recognize the first truths as 'clear and distinct', then God must have instituted them to appear as such: 'Because He willed that the three angles of a triangle are necessarily equal to two right angles, it is true' (that is, evident to us). The fundamental truths, then, are innate. If we cannot form a notion of a thing, that thing does not exist. Thus, in the last resort, human reason became the measuring-rod for the truth of existence! There cannot be a void, not because God could not have made it, but because He does not will it to be, and I know this because my reason cannot conceive how a void could possibly exist.

Man understands the world not (as in scholasticism) because of his analogy to God, but because of the fact that God does not want to deceive him. Of course, in practice the result was the same: man can construct a natural science in a deductive way in the same way as he has developed mathematics. Though God could make things that we do not understand, in fact He did not do so. Thus Descartes claimed to find the first principles of what is or what can be in the world from nothing but 'certain germs of truth that are by nature in our soul'.

Descartes, deviating from his original standpoint, even said that because God is immutable, the quantity of movement in the world must also remain constant; that is, he linked the reality of God's existence to the veracity of the law of constancy of momentum. It was not the will of God, but His very essence, which was the cause of this law, and it was by taking this point of view that Descartes' voluntarism changed into necessitarianism.

Descartes then deduced seven rules of collision and said that their demonstration was so certain that, if experience would seem to prove the contrary, 'we would be obliged to trust more in our reason than in our senses'. Unfortunately, six out of the seven rules, as well as his version of the fundamental law, turned out to be false. Yet he triumphantly declared at the end of his *Principia Philosophiae* 'that one has more than merely moral certainty that all things in the world are as we have proved here that they can be'. He even pretended to have deduced water, air, fire, minerals and other simple bodies, from the innate germs of truth. Of course, the result was a fantastic cosmogony which lacked any real scientific value. Its mathematical character (of which he boasted so much) consisted in its ontology, in its deductive method and in its geometrical models, but not

43

in a reliable description and interrelation of facts by mathematical formulae. His theories soon crumbled down before the critique of Huygens and Newton.

Huygens emphasized that Descartes was wrong in supposing that the fundamental notions of mechanics are wholly perspicuous to reason. And even Malebranche finally recognized that Descartes' linking of the law of constancy of the quantity of motion with God's immutability, infringed the freedom of God. In the opinion of the Oratorian priest this law was God's purely arbitrary choice and we could be sure of its truth only by a kind of revelation, that is, by experimental verification.[19]

D. EMPIRICIST OPPOSITION TO DESCARTES

Criticism of rationalistic pretensions will, of course, cut most deeply when it turns out that physical reality is *not* wholly conformable to what we, in a certain epoch, considered to be rational, and when the non-rationality, or even absurdity, of reality (or a part of reality) has to be acknowledged.[20] This insight was to come with Pascal and the English 'Christian Virtuosi'—Boyle, Hooke and Newton. These thinkers abandoned all Platonic pretensions about the ontological value of mathematics, and all *a priori* speculation as to which mathematical laws should prevail in nature.

a. *Pascal*

When Descartes rejected the void because otherwise some physical phenomena would be incomprehensible, Pascal retorted that it is quite possible to know a thing without understanding its nature. 'It is not by our capacity of understanding things that we have to judge about their truth'.[21] As long as we cannot demonstrate that there is some matter in Torricelli's space, it is empty *for us*.[22] It is, in Pascal's opinion, a natural disease of man to think that he always possesses the truth; it may be incomprehensible that light goes through empty space, but this does not give the philosophers a right to introduce imaginary fluids and causes in order to make nature comprehensible: 'in order to satisfy their vanity by the ruin of verity'.[23] In science things must be accepted as it pleased God to make them.

The analogy of the givenness of the natural world with that of religious revelation presented itself also to Pascal. In religion we are obliged to accept the way in which it pleased God to reveal Himself, that is, 'in Jesus Christ, without whom no communion with God is possible'. This may not correspond to the lofty ideas about the Godhead which human reason produced, but, 'how dares such a low being assume the right to put to God the limits that his own thought imposes on himself?'[24] To Pascal a divine revelation has to be accepted (or rejected), but it cannot be put in doubt just because it is not rational. In the same way in science hard facts have to be accepted, no matter whether they are or are not conformable to the expectations of reason. Thus, in spite of his strict methodological separation of Science and Theology, Pascal's scientific method strongly bears the stamp of his religious faith. He took up an empirical attitude towards both studies: that which *experience* has revealed (to me or to others), that which has been touched and seen, is the foundation of both. In physics, so he said, experience has more power to convince than has reason; experiments are the true teachers which one has to follow. Consequently, physics cannot be wholly perspicuous to reason.

Pascal denied that man has a clear understanding of the

fundamental notions of physics such as matter, space or gravitation, and he thought it an immense presumption to contend that one could explain all things with the help of scientific principles. Whereas according to Descartes these principles were perspicuous, Pascal considered them inevitable, but obscure. If Reason were really reasonable, he maintained, people would drop such pretensions; but he did not believe that reason would ever give up chasing the horizon. Yet Pascal was no irrationalist, for he considered reason to be the highest gift to man—'our whole dignity consists in thinking'. His critique was aimed at speculative reason, not at critical reason, and he felt that the final step in the process of reason was its acknowledgement that an infinity of things are beyond reason.[25]

b. *Boyle*

The English physicists, at about the same time, levelled a similar attack on rationalism, though perhaps with less profundity and vigour. The members of the Royal Society 'having before their eyes so many fatal Instances of the errors and falsehood, in which the greatest part of mankind has so long wandered because they rely'd upon the strength of human reason alone, have begun now to correct all Hypotheses by *sense*' (R. Hooke). These members considered themselves to be Baconians, and even Newton, though certainly not following Bacon in his neglect of mathematics, followed, according to Henry Pemberton, the true Baconian method—'the method of induction, on which all science is founded'. According to Robert Hooke, 'science has to begin with the Hands and Eyes, to be continued by the Reason, and to come back to the Hands and Eyes again'. He asked his readers not to consider his 'small conjectures' as irrefutable science, but as uncertain guesses.

Boyle, whose work for some time was closely connected with that of Hooke, assumed the same sceptical attitude. Though he also was a staunch defender of 'mechanistic philosophy', he emphasized, even more strongly, the experimental character of science. He considered that it is rational to abandon reasonable theories when experience contradicts them. In his opinion the contingency of nature takes away any character of logical necessity from science, as God freely established the laws of nature. In particular Boyle felt it wrong for Descartes to suppose he knew the extent of God's immutability so precisely that he could make it an *a priori* argument for his law of conservation of motion. The only certainty that could be introduced into this argument was that experience is not against it. Man should not ask what God could do, but what He really did do. Boyle made the acute remark that the exclusive truth of mechanical philosophy could not be proved: it was acceptable because it brought divergent phenomena into a coherent relationship.

Boyle clearly did not consider the fundamental notions even of his own mechanistic philosophy to be perspicuous to reason. In opposition to Descartes, he did not believe that the human mind is wholly adapted to the created order. He saw that our thoughts about space, matter and atoms, for instance, could lead to absurdities and that we are unable to give satisfactory definitions of these concepts. Yet the physicist can work with them, and Boyle rightly considered one of the differences between a speculative and an experimental philosopher to be that the latter is willing to use even concepts which he does not fully understand.

In our own age, too, some of the greatest scientists have occupied themselves with the investigation of fundamentals and they have come to the same way of thinking as Pascal, Boyle and Newton, those fathers of modern science, who in the end felt that they could only 'lay their hand upon their mouth'.

Boyle considered science to be an excellent school for religion. He pointed out that both science and religion are based on fundamentals that are incomprehensible, and that both are founded on facts 'historical' rather than rationally cogent. The scientist finds much in nature that he does not thoroughly understand, and he has therefore a special aptitude for accepting things that seem to be beyond belief to the 'vulgar philosopher'—the man who thinks that he understands all things and that nothing which does not conform to his philosophy could be true. The scientist is prepared to learn even from unlearned people; just as it would be possible to learn more about the natural history of America from a companion of Columbus than from a hundred Schoolmen, so too one could learn more about God from those unlearned men, the apostles, who were in close contact with 'Him who was at the heart of the Father', than from any philosopher.[26]

In Boyle's opinion experimental, empirical science is an ally of religion, and even guided by it, despite the methodological separation between the two. Hostility exists only between speculative metaphysics on the one side and religion-cum-true-science on the other. Boyle, especially in his *Christian Virtuoso*, gives much attention to this topic of the parallels between science and religion. Neither has any use for 'innate ideas'; both recognize that our limited intellect can form right notions only with the help of the patterns offered in 'the *works* and the *verdicts* of God'; it is only in this way that we can know that the ideas of the ancient son both issues were wrong.[27]

c. *Newton*

Finally, Isaac Newton made an effort to combine Baconian experimentation and empiricism with the mathematical method. In the Preface to his *Philosophiae Naturalis Principia Mathematica* (1687) he had already revealed his empiricism: 'I offer this work as the mathematical principles of philosophy, for the whole burden of philosophy seems to consist in this—from the phenomena of motions to investigate the forces of nature, and then from these forces to demonstrate the other phenomena'. Newton's empiricism, like that of Bacon, Pascal, Hooke and Boyle, had a theological background. The voluntaristic character of his thought becomes evident in Cotes' preface to the second edition of the *Principia*: 'Without all doubt this world . . . could arise from nothing but the perfectly free will of God. . . . From this fountain . . . (what) we call the laws of nature have flowed, in which there appear many traces indeed of the most wise contrivance, but not the least shadow of necessity. These therefore we must not seek from uncertain conjectures, but learn them from observations and experiments. He who is presumptuous enough to think that he can find the true principles of physics and the laws of natural things by the force alone of his own mind, and the internal light of reason, must either suppose that the world exists by necessity, and by the same necessity follows the laws proposed; or, if the order of Nature was established by the will of God, that himself, a miserable reptile, can tell what was fittest to be done'. The first thrust is levelled at the Greeks, the second at Descartes.

Newton never made such sweeping claims for his system as Descartes had made for his philosophy. He did not consider gravitation to be the universal cause in physics. Yet his disciples showed an undue tendency to generalize, and to make absolute not only his results but also his tentative conjectures. The poet Cowley called Bacon the Moses who showed the Promised Land, and Newton the Joshua who entered into it, and Pope even declared that through Newton 'all was light'. Newton himself, however, was more modest when in his old age he recognized the limitations of his understanding, saying: 'I do not know what I may appear to the world, but to myself I seem to have been only a boy playing on the seashore, and diverting myself in now and then finding a smoother pebble or a prettier shell than ordinary, while the great ocean of truth lay all undiscovered before me'.

Perhaps it may seem not so strange after all that the adherents of the new experimental or mechanical philosophy considered themselves the Christian virtuosi, and this in spite of the fact that, in Bacon's wake, they were protagonists of a separation of science from divinity. The defenders of the old scholastic philosophy accused them of undermining religion, and of introducing materialistic principles instead of the approved, more spiritual, principles of Form, essence, Idea and purpose. They themselves, however, considered their secularization of science to be its christianisation, because they had freed science from the human authority of theologians and philosophers and from the oppressive burden of its old idols, named Forms and Ideas. This came about precisely because they kept obediently to the Book of Creatures, written, as they firmly believed, by God Himself. When they stressed the contingency of nature and the always unfinished character of natural science, they were putting forward biblical conceptions. Without borrowing scientific data from Holy Scripture, they were yet convinced that it had made their science truly free. Boyle expresses their point of view when he says: 'The revealed truths, if they be burdens to reason, are but such burdens as feathers are to a hawk, which, instead of hindering his flight by their weight, enable him to soar toward heaven, and take a larger prospect than, if he had no feathers, he could possibly do'.

d. *Retrospect*

Looking back we can see that the methodological controversy in science led to a victory of rational empiricism over rationalism, and that the former found a support in voluntaristic theology. Rational empiricism recognized that Man, as the image of God, could find a certain order in nature, but that he had also to accept reality even when it did not appear rational to him. The difference between the views represented by Descartes on the one hand, and those of Newton on the other, was succinctly expressed by Fontenelle (the secretary of the Académie des Sciences) when he said that the one started from what he clearly understood in order to find the causes of what he saw, whereas the other started from what he saw in order to find the causes whether clear or obscure.

Many protagonists of modern science recognized the parallel between their religious and their scientific-methodological conceptions. Francis Bacon referred to this when pointing out that in order to arrive at a truly reliable science, it is necessary first to become as a little child; Sprat said the same when he suggested as characteristics of a Christian and of a scientist that both have a certain distrust in their own thoughts; and in the nineteenth century even that agnostic in religion, T. H. Huxley, repeated this point when he said: 'Science seems to me to teach in the highest and strongest manner the great truth which is embodied in the Christian conception of entire surrender to the will of God: Sit down

E   51

before fact as a little child, be prepared to give up every preconceived notion, follow humbly and to whatever abysses nature leads, or you shall learn nothing'.[28]

NOTES TO CHAPTER II

1. Isaiah 55:8, 9.
2. 1 Corinthians 1:23.
3. Luke 24:39; John 20:25-29; 1 John 1:1.
4. Change, according to Aristotle, is the transition from the potential to the actual, from being-possible to being-real.
5a. On Tempier, Buridan and Oresme, cf. R. Hooykaas, *Science and Theology in the Middle Ages*, Free University Quarterly, 3 (1954), pp. 77-163.
5b. Cf. Ch. I, p. 17, where we find the same question with Basso (1621), and p. 21, Malebranche.
6. Nicole Oresme, *Le Livre du ciel et du monde*, ii, 95a.
7. See above, Ch. I, p. 13.
8. In principle, the nominalists dropped the essential difference between heavenly and terrestrial motions and between natural and unnatural (violent) movements.
9. J. Kepler, *De fundamentis astrologiae certioribus* (1601), thesis XX.
9b. Cf. R. Hooykaas, *The Impact of the Voyages of Discovery on Portuguese Humanist Literature* (I Reuniao da Historia da Nautica, October 1968), Revista Univ. Coimbra, (1970).
10. Tycho Brahe, *Astronomiae Instauratae Progymnasmata*, P. ii, Cap. 3.
11. B. Pascal, *Traités de l'équilibre des liqueurs et de la pesanteur de la masse de l'air*. Conclusion.
12. B. Palissy, *Discours admirable* (1580). Avertissement aux lecteurs.
13. D. João de Castro, *Tratado da sphaera*, in: *Obras completas de D. João de Castro*, ed. crit. por A. Cortesao e L.de Albuquerque, Coimbra, 1968, vol. i, p. 58.
14. Isaac Beeckman, *Journal*, ed. C. de Waard, vol. ii, p. 100 (Aug. 1620). Cf. R. Hooykaas, *Science and Religion in the Seventeenth Century*; *Isaac Beeckman*, in Free Univ. Qu., 1 (1951), pp. 169-183.
14a. F. Bacon, *The Advancement of Learning* (1605), Bk. I.
15. In the Middle Ages, the Nominalists; in the seventeenth century Pascal, Boyle, Newton.
16. In the Middle Ages, the Idealists and the Realists.
17. R. Descartes, *Meditationes*, 3d ed. (1650), *Sextae responsiones*.

Reason and Experience

18. Descartes, *Meditationes, Quintae responsiones*. Cf. Malebranche, above Ch. I, p. 21.
19. Strangely enough, Malebranche remained more rationalistic than Descartes when maintaining the eternal truth of mathematical fundamentals independently of the will of God.
20. Cf. above, Beeckman and de Castro.
21. Pascal, *Pensées*, fr. 233. On Pascal Cf. R. Hooykaas, *Pascal, his Science and his Religion*, in: Free Univ. Qu., 2 (1952), pp. 106–137.
22. Pascal, *Expériences nouvelles touchant le vide* (1647).
23. Pascal, *Traités*, Conclusion.
24. Pascal, *Pensées*, fr. 430.
25. Pascal, *Pensées*, fr. 267.
26. R. Boyle, *The Christian Virtuoso*, First Part, prop. II, 2.
27. Boyle, *The Christian Virtuoso*, First Part, prop. II.
28. T. H. Huxley to Ch. Kingsley, Sept. 23, 1860.

CHAPTER III

NATURE AND ART

A. THE CONTRAST BETWEEN ART AND NATURE

a. Techne *incapable of equalling* Physis

Techne (art), in its original meaning, covered the making of laws as well as skill in measuring and counting; the drawing of pictures as well as the baking of bread. We will concentrate our attention, however, on technology in its modern sense, considered as an applied science of nature, as the attainment of dominion over nature in order to put her to the service of man. In this connection, our ancestors were confronted with three problems. Is the artificer able to do what nature does? Is the artificer permitted to try to do what nature does? Finally, should art be left to the artificers or should the scholar also occupy himself with the subject? In other words the question was whether the natural philosopher could, should or would imitate and dominate nature.

At first the problem of *physis* and *techne* was mainly concerned with ethics and law. To some Greek philosophers nature represented nothing more than the elements moved by blind necessity (*ananke*) or by chance (*tyche*). They set this necessity of nature over against law (*nomos*) and religion, which they considered to be merely arbitrary institutions, depending on human caprice and on time and place. These were 'arts', which go against nature, and were therefore inferior to her.

Plato, in strong protest against such impious conceptions, reversed the order and taught that law (*nomos*) and art (*techne*) are the true nature and that they are the origin of all

54

things. So the visible world is a product of the art of the world soul, who directs the dumb elements, which are thus subject to art and to *logos*[1] and which are not 'Nature' in the proper sense. The emphasis on the concept of Nature as an artificer was shifted by other idealistic philosophers such as Aristotle and Galen, from moral and political law to physics. They compared the *logos* of the world with an artificer, an architect, a cook, a potter, a painter, a carpenter; that is, they believed that Nature carries out a plan. This primacy of art, however, did not mean that human art could be superior to that of Nature. On the contrary, although the image of the artificer had been borrowed from that of the human artificer, in fact they considered the latter to be but a faint shadow of the Great Artificer, Nature. 'Art imitates Nature'. The human arts, as Aristotle said, '*either* on the basis of Nature bring things further than Nature could do' (as in agriculture), '*or* they imitate Nature'[2] (as in spinning). This idea that the arts took their origin from an imitation of Nature was a popular theme with the poets and philosophers of antiquity. Democritus said that the spider taught us spinning and weaving, and the swallow building. Lucretius thought that the art of cooking was inspired by the sun; while, according to Vitruvius, observation of the rotating heavens led to the making of machines.

The ancient notion of Nature, especially that of Aristotle, had both a *rationalistic* and a *vitalistic* aspect.[3] Only the former had any comparison with the activity of the artificers, for both the artificer and Nature worked according to *logos* and to a plan. As far as the latter aspect was concerned, however, natural things only have their principle of motion and growth towards the fullness of their being or Form within themselves, while artificial things, on the other hand, receive their form and their motions from some external cause. That is, natural things arise through *generation* by means of a similar thing, artificial things by *fabrication*. Cicero spoke for all the ancients when he said that no art, no hand, no artificer, could equal the skill of Nature by imitation.[4]

b. *The illegitimacy of competing with Nature*

The idea that it is impossible to compete with Nature through art was mainly a theme of the philosophers, whereas the theologians and the poets made the point that such competition is in fact illicit. They argued that if Nature is divine, man is claiming divine prerogatives when he pretends to do her work. Such an act would be trespassing on the bounds of a realm that Nature (or fate, or a god), had reserved for herself and it would be a violation of *moira*, the eternal world order. The penalty for intrusion into that realm is divine vengeance. Prometheus, who stole fire from the gods, was duly punished by the Lord of Heaven; Salmoneus, 'the audacious and godless' as Vergil called him, who tried to mimic thunder and 'inimitable lightning', was struck by the flashes of lightning of the 'almighty Father'.

The artificial was considered inferior to the natural, even from a moral point of view. This was emphasized in stories about the Golden Age, when man still lived soberly and, as Seneca would have it, without architects, carpenters and weavers, or, as Lucretius thought, even without agriculture, and when everybody was healthy and contented.

c. *The Influence of the Separation of Art and Nature on Mechanics and Chemistry*

The effect of this antagonism between Nature and art was felt especially in the fields of chemistry and of mechanics. In chemistry any effort to make something equivalent to a natural product was considered to be doomed beforehand to failure, as man could *generate* only man, whereas he could at best *fabricate* other things by giving them *artificial* Forms. Mechanics, too, could be seen to work against Nature, as for example when heavy burdens were lifted by small forces. The words *mechane* and *machina* meant an instrument, but were also used to signify craftiness. Pappus (third century) wrote that mechanicians who occupied themselves with pneumatics and automata were called wonder-workers (*thaumatourgoi*). Because mechanics went against Nature, apparently trying to cheat her, it was considered that this science must therefore have connections with magic, the effort to subdue Nature. The oldest alchemical manuscript which has survived shows drawings of distillation apparatus as well as formulae for conjuring up the heavenly bodies and the serpent, which symbolizes the cycle of Nature.

The ancient conception of the relation of Nature and art survived into the Middle Ages. At that time only the alchemists pretended to go beyond this and to change one species, lead, into another, gold. Jean de Meung wrote that 'alchemy is a true art . . . which makes gold from silver'. The argument against this idea of art was that anything capable of generation, generates something similar to itself— the Form, essence or soul of lead, cannot produce the Form of gold; an ass does not give birth to a horse. So what Nature cannot do is quite beyond the reach of art to achieve.

The absolute reign of eternal Forms, however, had been directly attacked by Bishop Tempier when he condemned the thesis that God could not create new Forms.[5] A further weakening of the rigidity of the doctrine of Forms was the belief of the nominalists of the fourteenth century that species—and also the Forms determining them—are but abstractions, names for groups of similar individuals, which are the only things with a real, concrete existence. Consequently the distinction between natural and artificial Forms became less important.

This anti-Aristotelian trend was even more evident in the doctrine of 'latitudes'. According to the nominalist Heinrich von Langenstein, other proportions and other treatments of the same materials could produce new Forms. He expected that God would go on creating new species in the future, and that if God was not bound to pre-existent eternal Forms, the same could be said to be true for His image, man. The snag, however, was that there are an infinity of proportions and an infinity of possible treatments, so that it was virtually impossible to hit upon the combination of these which was required, for instance, for the production of gold. At any rate, though in practice it would be well-nigh impossible, in principle it was conceivable that a 'natural' substance might be made by an artificial procedure. Of course the atomic theory, which wholly rejected substantial Forms, could lead to these same conclusions, as some nominalists, Oresme for instance, clearly recognized.

The alchemists followed another line of reasoning. They claimed that their imitation of Nature was perfect and that their artificial gold could not be distinguished from the natural. In general, they did not pretend that their fabrication by art equalled the generation by Nature, but they referred rather to the other procedure of art mentioned by Aristotle.[6] The artificial procedures of the alchemists were said merely to help and support Nature in full accomplishment of the design, which she had already partly completed, of realizing the perfect Form. That process which Nature usually requires 1000 years to achieve, art tried to accelerate, so that the whole could be perfected in a few weeks. The implication here was that there was no real transmutation of

Forms; lead was considered to be an imperfect *variety* of the metal that manifested its full Form as gold. Some alchemists, including Geber in the thirteenth century, went further and showed a tendency to move towards the corpuscular theory of matter. Geber boldly declared that the difference between gold and lead is accidental; the transmutation of the latter into the former consists in changing the proportions of the elements and in taking away impurities. He even declared that Nature's species were not always fixed, and that when a worm turns into a fly, there was a transmutation of species. Why then would it be too presumptuous to help Nature to turn lead into gold?[7]

The nominalists challenged not only the pretended monopoly of the production of Forms, but also other prerogatives of Nature. The essential distinction between natural and violent motions was effaced by applying the same impetus theory to the fall of bodies, a natural motion, as to the projection of bodies, which was an unnatural motion, and even the rotation of a millstone was treated as analogous with that of the heavens.

d. *Paracelsus*

Theophrastus Paracelsus (1493–1541), in particular, greatly helped to efface the borderline between Art and Nature. He pointed out that all artificial procedures are founded on natural ones and he thus emphasized that aspect of Art which was seen as perfecting and helping Nature. He took his examples not only from agriculture but also from the work of such artisans as bakers, carpenters and shoemakers. Above all, however, Paracelsus chose the alchemist as his model. Here, perhaps for the first time, an academic took the side of those people who, in the eyes of scholastic philosophers, were trying to do that which could not be done, that which should not be done, and that which was, moreover, beneath the dignity of a true scholar to do at all. The alchemists themselves, in spite of all these objections, had always claimed that their 'art' was also a 'science', a philosophy. They proudly and defiantly called themselves 'philosophers through fire'. Paracelsus now backed them up, saying that fire, whether put to work in distillation, forging or cooking, was the paramount means used both by Nature and by art for perfecting their works.

e. *Art surpassing Nature*

The general belief in the Middle Ages was that the feats of Nature could be surpassed only by magic. Roger Bacon, who lived in the thirteenth century, pointed out, however, that many seemingly impossible things are possible to the artificer, although those who know how these things are done admit that the effects are obtained by putting the powers of Nature at the service of man. Bacon felt that such natural magic is perfectly lawful, but even so he was considered to be a sorcerer, as any efforts on the part of man to equal Nature or to surpass her were thought impious. Bacon, on the other hand, proudly declared that it was possible for man to make a mixture that could produce thunder and lightning more tremendous than those of the natural powers. During the Renaissance especially, this 'natural magic' prepared the way for the rapid development of scientific experiment in the seventeenth century; the word 'experimentum' covered the practice of witchcraft as well as that of scientific experimentation.

B. THE ABOLITION OF THE CONTRAST BETWEEN NATURE AND ART

a. *The Transition from the Organistic to the Mechanistic Concept*

The beginning of the seventeenth century marked a turning point in the appreciation of art as compared with nature. Even the very conservative Spanish Jesuit Martin del Rio (1599), who scented diabolic magic in every corner, showed a certain good-will towards chemistry. Of course, he considered this art as an extension or as a support of nature, but he recognized the possibility of transmutation of species, as according to him this also occurs in nature. He took the view that vitriol (copper sulphate) made in the laboratory does not differ from that produced by nature.[8] He was not willing, however, to make the next step and he continued to maintain that substances made by art, which did not occur in nature, could not possibly be products of 'Nature'. Here scholastic prejudice prevented him from making any further progress.

A more complete abandonment of the distinction between art and nature could only appear with the triumph of the mechanistic world picture. In the Greek conception, the art exercised by Nature was a non-conscious and inimitable self-reproduction, bound to her eternal immanent Forms. In the Christian conception, on the other hand, nature is, as Thomas Browne put it, the art of God, and this art of God is adumbrated in human art precisely as God's absolute free will is shadowed forth in man's relatively free will.

According to the French author Henri de Monantheuil (1599), God is a mechanician and his work is a mechanism—'The world is a machine; it is the most purposeful and beautiful instrument'. He maintains that man is a mechanician because he is the image of God; man knows, however, that God is a mechanician, because man is one. The great difference is, that God did not need any instrument, as He created His work by willing it.[9]

It was not easy to abandon the organic world picture and to accept the mechanistic one. William Gilbert (1600) thought that it was a degradation of the world to deny to it a soul, because if the earth brought forth living beings, it must itself also be alive; if even the worms have a kind of soul, so must the earth also. To consider God as a mechanician and the world as a mechanism seemed to him to be disparaging to both.

Kepler had the greatest difficulty in changing over from the one view to the other. In 1597 he held to the organistic view; in 1605 he was arguing that the world machine should be explained not after the example of a divine animal but after that of a clock. In 1619 he had returned to the discarded view of an animate world, maintaining that there are planet souls and that the earth is a living being that breathes. In 1621 he came back again to the mechanistic conception, which in his life story seems to be associated with renewed efforts to make mechanical models of the world.

Gilbert and Kepler however, were typical transition figures; the more radical philosophical innovator Isaac Beeckman rejected as valueless all the arguments of Copernicus, Gilbert and Kepler which appealed to the beauty, dignity and simplicity of the universe. The idea of an animated earth appeared to him 'unworthy for a natural scientist'.

b. *Francis Bacon's Advocacy of the Power of Art*

If man has been made after the image of God, he can

reasonably be expected to be able to make at least some of
the things which God has made. Whereas the Greeks felt
that to command Nature was to attempt the impossible, as
even the gods were obliged to respect the law of necessity,
the biblical authors believed that God has conferred some of
His divine power of command on the highest of His creatures.
Thus the hard and fast dividing line between the natural and
the artificial became blurred through the influence of biblical teaching.

This influence is perhaps even more evident in that it
reverses the ethical evaluation of attempts to dominate
nature by human *techne*. The Greeks saw any effort to compete with Nature in making her products as an impiety
(*hubris*) or at least as an audacity; in the biblical view, however, dominion over his fellow-creatures is granted to Man.
On the other hand, whereas to the Greeks it was no *hubris*
to think that man could have a full understanding of God's
works, to the biblical authors such an idea is highly presumptuous.

In this connection, it is important to remember that
Francis Bacon (1561–1626), the herald of modern science,
defended the new view on *techne* even before the mechanistic philosophy became triumphant. The two pillars of
Hercules, the symbols of the ancient *non ultra* (no further),
signified for him the *over*-estimation of ancient science and
the *under*-estimation of the possibility of surpassing it. The
title-page of his *Great Instauration* (1620) bears a drawing of
a ship passing between these pillars, which bear the inscrip-
tion *plus ultra* (still further). For, in imitation of the heavens,
men had circumnavigated the earth, and instead of the
'inimitable lightning' of the ancients, the moderns might
speak of the 'imitable lightning'.[10] These two examples
were given by Bacon to demonstrate that man is able to

compete with heavenly as well as with terrestrial nature. Discoveries, said Bacon, are, so to speak, new creations and imitations of God's works. In his opinion the dominion of man over things wholly depends on the arts and the sciences; man ought no longer to follow Aristotle in despairing of the power of art to compete with nature; there was no reason to think that artificial fire could not do the same things as the sun, or that man could make only mixtures and no true compounds. Bacon also forcefully rejected Aristotle's opinion that art can only be the hand-maid of Nature and help her to finish what she has already begun. He held that on the contrary man could lead the motions of bodies in such a way that, on the basis of nature, art could make the same things that nature could bring forth without assistance. The difference between Aristotle's and Bacon's artificial help to nature was evidently that for Aristotle man helps Nature's immanent urge to overcome outward difficulties as well as her own weakness, whereas Bacon argued that natural forces and things are simply *directed* according to a human plan. In the Aristotelian conception one can help Nature only in fulfilling her own designs, whereas Francis Bacon wants to use nature to fulfil the design of Man.

With Bacon the potentialities of art were enlarged be-cause the idea of generation was abandoned for that of the fabrication of natural things. He denied any essential dis-tinction between natural and artificial movements in mechanics, or between natural and artificial production (or between generation and fabrication) in chemistry. In this way the history (description) of mechanical arts became for him a part of the history of nature and could even be en-titled 'History of Nature wrought or Mechanical'.[11] So there was no real contradiction in Bacon's emphasis on the one hand on the dominion of man over nature, and in his maintaining on the other that man ought obediently to follow nature; for 'nature cannot be commanded except by being obeyed'. The argument was that it is impossible to go beyond the potentialities of nature, but these potentialities are much greater than one would expect if nature were left to herself. In order to be successful, however, human interference with nature has to be in conformity with the fundamental laws of nature; it has to be founded, therefore, on a reliable knowledge of nature. 'And so those twin objects, human knowledge and human power, do really meet in one; and it is from ignorance of causes that operation fails'.[12]

The rejection of an essential difference between natural and artificial forms led Bacon to predict great feats of human technology. In his *New Atlantis* he said that natural compounds might be artificially made, and new metals produced; it was possible that botanical species would undergo transmutation, that new animal species be bred, artificial changes of climate be wrought, and all this 'not by chance but by knowledge, according to plan'.

c. *The Artificial Synthesis of Natural Compounds*

It is remarkable that precisely at the time when Bacon made these predictions, natural compounds had in fact been made by artificial procedures. Angelo Sala demonstrated in 1617 the identity of some artificial and natural compounds.[13] In the opinion of the Aristotelians artificial compounds were but mock compounds; they had no unity but they were just appositions of the particles of the components, without a 'Form' of their own. Natural compounds, on the other hand, were considered to be perfectly homogeneous and to possess their own nature and Form. Now, the more it became possible to synthesize natural compounds in the laboratory, the more the distinction between the products of art and those of nature lost its meaning, and the more the mechanistic interpretation of chemical compounds enlarged its field of application. Thus chemistry, on its own account, without the help of philosophy, gradually abandoned the substantial Forms. Of course the theoretical opposition of 'mechanical philosophy' to the doctrine of substantial Forms was a welcome ally. Boyle, for example, used both methods, that of experimentation and that of the rational critique of Greek philosophy, to support each other. The organic world picture hardly admitted that natural compounds could be made by art, whereas the mechanistic philosophy, in which generation is in fact a kind of fabrication, almost invited the conclusion that art (*mechane*) must be able to make at least some of the things that nature produces.

d. *Mechanicism and Technology*

As might be expected, from now on, instead of the over-emphasis on man's inability to compete with nature, exaggerated claims were made for the capacity of human art. To Descartes even plants and animals are mere mechanisms: 'There is no difference at all between the machines that the artificers make, and the bodies nature makes on her own account'; 'all rules valid in mechanics are valid in physics, so that things artificial are also natural'. 'It is as natural for a watch to indicate the time by means of its wheels, as it is for a tree to bear fruit'. Analogy between organism and mechanism had here become identity. On the other hand, Descartes supposed animals and plants to be such complicated machines that it would be impossible for man ever to construct them.

Monantholius had already (in 1599) asserted that the world

mechanism is more perfect than the machines made by man in so far as its Maker Himself is more perfect than man. The new view, nevertheless, abolished the absolute and essential distinction between products of nature and art; according to Robert Hooke the difference in skill is immense, but for him this does not imply that it is essential. At any rate, whereas formerly 'mechanics' meant 'applied mathematics' and was a manual art, and physics was a contemplative philosophy about the essence (nature, *physis*) of things, henceforth mechanics was to be the most fundamental part of experimental physics, for which it provided the manipulations as well as the theoretical basis. The mechanisation of the world picture abolished the opposition between nature and art.

C. THE DOMINION OF MAN OVER NATURE

a. *The Religious Vindication of the Right and the Duty to dominate Nature*

The biblical conception of nature liberated man from the naturalistic bonds of Greek religiosity and philosophy and gave a religious sanction to the development of technology, that is, to the dominion of nature by human art. Though the mechanistic world picture is not contained in the bible, yet it shares in common with the biblical concept the fact that it implies a de-deification of nature. This took away the obstacles caused by its deification by the ancients and made it possible to accept not only that man *could* compete with nature or even surpass her, but that he *should* do so. No prohibition now existed, and the numinous holy character of nature had vanished. Man may be unable to find out all the works of God, nevertheless he had been set the difficult task of trying to do so,[14] with, in addition, the right and the duty to dominate nature. In a time when, as in the sixteenth and seventeenth centuries, religious sanction was indispensable in order to make a thing flourish, science and technology profited greatly from this change of outlook.

Francis Bacon clearly saw that man's adoration of nature was a great impediment to the dominion of man over the lower creatures: 'Many have not only considered it to be impossible but also as something impious to try to efface the bounds nature seems to put to her works'. In Bacon's opinion God has made us His fellow-workers and given us the commandment to investigate His works. He even thought that God had pre-ordained the coincidence of the geographical discoveries (the new *material* globe) with the beginning of a new science (the *intellectual* globe), in accordance with the words of the prophet Daniel: 'Many shall go to and fro, and knowledge shall be increased'.

According to Bacon there are two sources of theological error: that of ignoring the *will* of God, revealed in Scripture, and that of ignoring the *power* of God, revealed or made visible in His creatures.[15] We ought not, out of fear that scientific investigation might lead to a lack of reverence for God's revelation, to fall into the opposite error of thinking 'that investigation of any part of nature should be forbidden'. It is wrong to transfer the prohibition against a too curious penetration into the mysteries of God's being, to the investigation of the mysteries of nature, for nowhere in Scripture is this forbidden; nay, said Bacon, it is even encouraged. The first fall, in his opinion, was not a consequence of a too great desire for knowledge of nature; it was a consequence of man's wanting to establish the law of good and evil instead of following the revelation of the will of God. God left to man the dominion over nature, but this was lost through a second fall, 'because we wanted again to be as God, and to follow the dictates of our own reason'.

There is a remarkable contrast here again between the old and the new attitudes. In Antiquity and the Middle Ages a too great confidence in the human capacity for understanding nature went together with a sense of despair about the weakness of the *power* of man over nature. In the sixteenth and seventeenth centuries, on the contrary, the new humility with regard to the depth of scientific knowledge grew side by side with an almost boundless optimism as to technological possibilities. Kepler considered that as soon as the art of flying had been invented, a colony of men would be established on the moon. John Wilkins reminds his readers that the ancients thought the first man who ventured on the sea too bold, and he goes on: 'now, how easy a thing is this even to a timorous and cowardly nature'. He adds that 'without any doubt some means of conveyance to the moon cannot seem more incredible to us, than overseas navigation to the ancients, and that therefore there is no good reason to be discouraged in our hope of the like success'.[16]

b. *Scientific Research as a Duty of Charity*

Bacon feared that the new science would lead to a new *hubris* and a new fall, if it did not develop side by side with charity, for 'knowledge puffs up, but charity edifies'[17]; to him the kingdom of man is closely tied up with the kingdom of God. The new science means the restoration of our dominion over nature which we have lost by our second fall; it means a purification of the intellect from all its pride and misconceptions; it is a humble acceptance of what has been given in nature, 'for the entering into the Kingdom of Man, founded on the Sciences, does not differ very much from the entering into the Kingdom of Heaven, where nobody can enter, except as a little child'. Thus, Bacon's divorce between science and *theology* was no divorce of science from *religion*. On the contrary, the core of his prophetic message of the kingdom of man was his faith in the kingdom of God.

Mankind in Bacon's time lived in a continual fear of the powers of nature. Though in Christian theory nature had no divine power, she had kept it in practice and in general belief. Inundation, drought, hunger, disease and pestilence visited man as irresistible natural disasters, and although the birth rate was high, so too was the death rate. In Isaac Beeckman's diary we read how his children, one after another, died early; how an epidemic which was never chronicled claimed a quarter of the population of Dordrecht, and how his brothers succumbed one by one to consumption. He noted his own slowly diminishing weight, until the last entry in the diary, made by his younger and only surviving brother, told that Beeckman too had died of consumption. The sad wording of the baptismal service of the Netherlands Reformed Churches, which speaks about 'this life which is but a continual death' was not an expression of the gloominess of Calvinism, as some people think to-day, but of the reality of the times. Even so, some of the pictures of Holland's Golden Age in the museums of the Netherlands bear testimony to the fortitude and gaiety which could prevail in spite of grief. During this period the physicist Willebrord Snel lost fourteen of the seventeen children of his two marriages; he was survived by only three of them and two of these died young. In England, the theologian John Owen (1616–1683) lost ten of his eleven children when they were quite small. The scientist Conrad Gesner, a friend of Bullinger, died of the pest in 1567 together with about 3700 of the 6000 inhabitants of Zurich. Medical science often made the situation worse instead of

better, as in the case of Dr. Boate, the friend of Boyle and
Hartlieb, who died while 'being let blood by those common butchers of mankind' (Hartlieb, 1653). Thus, mankind
lived an unprotected life, not nearly as idyllic as some
pessimistic prophets of our own time would like us to
believe.

Francis Bacon, then, had reason to be seriously disturbed
about the danger, the pain and the toils of contemporary
life. He pointed out how insignificant had been the progress
of medical science since the time of the Greeks, how hard
was the labour of the vast majority of men, and how poorly
they could feed and clothe themselves in spite of all their
efforts. He blew the trumpet in the war against the sins of
laziness, despair, pride and ignorance and he urged his
contemporaries, for the sake of God and their neighbours,
to re-assume the rights that God had given them and to
restore that dominion over nature which God had allotted
to man. It was not the love of philosophical novelties, but
moral indignation, which inspired his crusade against the
scholastics. Their old 'science' did not bear fruit, it did not
alleviate the burden of life, because it separated art from
nature and put the Forms beyond the reach of man. But as in
Bacon's opinion a natural philosophy that stuck to words
and did not lead to works was as dead as a faith without
works, so too should science be directed towards the benefit
of man, for 'though I speak with the tongues of men and
angels and have not charity, I am as a tinkling cymbal'.[18]
His ideal was a science in the service of man, as the result of
the restoration of the rule of man over nature. This to him
was not a purely human but a divinely inspired work: 'The
beginning is from God . . . the Father of Lights'.[19] He concluded the preface to his *Historia Naturalis* with a prayer:
'May God, the Founder, Preserver, and Renewer of the

Universe, in His love and compassion to men, protect the work both in its ascent to His glory and its descent to the good of Man, through His only Son, God-with-us'.

Thus, modern technology, that is, a technology closely connected with science, found its most eloquent advocate in a man who placed it on a decidedly Christian basis, and it is quite understandable that the Puritans of the Commonwealth, who expected to establish the kingdom of God on earth, considered Bacon's kingdom of Man an integral part of it.

c. *Romantic Disapproval of Francis Bacon*

Bacon was highly esteemed by the poets of the Enlightenment, but at the end of the eighteenth century some of the romantic poets were less enthusiastic. According to William Blake 'Bacon's philosophy has ruined England'; 'the great Bacon he is called; I call him the little Bacon'; 'Bacon's philosophy has destroyed art and science'. In our own time no less a person than the late C. S. Lewis[20] has raised a vigorous protest against Baconian technology. In his opinion magic and applied science share a common ground in that they both try to *subdue* reality to the wishes of man in a situation where the solution was technique, whereas the wisdom of earlier ages saw as its problem how to *reconcile* the soul to reality, and here the solution had been recognized as knowledge, self-discipline and virtue. Strangely enough, this scholar, who was a convinced Christian, condemned human dominion over nature as being *hubris*, whereas he praised the ancient 'wisdom' of conforming to nature, although this had been a wisdom of the Stoics rather than of the Christians.

In Lewis' opinion there was a striking similarity between Bacon, 'the chief trumpeter of the modern era', and

Marlowe's Faust, who said that 'a sound magician is a mighty god' and that 'all things that move between the quiet poles shall be at his command'. Bacon's aim was to extend man's power to the performance of all things possible.

However, one might well ask whether knowledge for its own sake was always such a lofty thing. Not only technological science, but also 'la science pour la science' (science for its own sake), could be a 'science sans conscience'. Moreover, when two people say the same, they do not always mean the same. Marlowe's Faust wanted power for his own benefit; Bacon wanted it in obedience to the second injunction of the Law: that is to help *all* people. And, finally, Bacon stressed that the highest aim was not profit, nor power, nor any of these 'inferior things'; it was charity towards our fellow-men that should urge us to reform the sciences.

Bacon clearly saw that a purely utilitarian science would be of little use. If scientists concentrated on application, without first establishing a solid basis of pure science, they were going up a blind alley, and people who do that, 'as Atalanta they break off their course in order to get the golden apple and so they miss victory'. Again and again he stressed that the goal of alleviating the miseries of human life could not be reached without a true scientific knowledge: 'the contemplation of the light is higher than all the fruit of invention'. He did not choose between science and its useful applications; to him they were as indissolubly connected as faith and works: 'the works are even more to be estimated as tokens of truth than as contributions to the commodities of life'.

We cannot therefore agree with Lewis' verdict that 'the modern scientific movement was born in unhealthy surroundings and at an inauspicious hour'. It is true that the results of our dominion over nature have been unhealthy in many cases; the powerful river of modern science and technology has often caused disastrous inundations. But by comparison the contemplative, almost medieval, vision that is offered as an alternative would be a stagnant pool.

NOTES TO CHAPTER III

1. Plato, *Laws*, 892 B.C. The topic of this lecture has also been dealt with in *La Nature et l'art*, in: *Revista Fac. de Ciências da Univ. de Coimbra*, 39 (1967), pp. 1–26.
2. Aristotle, *Physics*, ii. 8, 199a.
3. See above, Ch. I, p. 11.
4. Cicero, *De Natura Deorum*, i. 33.
5. Cf. Ch. II, p. 32.
6. Cf. above, p. 55.
7. Geber, *Summa perfectionis magisterii*, lib. I, pars 2, c. 11.
8. Martinus del Rio, S.J., *Disquisitionum magicarum lib. VI*, Lib. I, c. 5, qu. 1, sect. 3.
9. Henricus Monantholius, *Aristotelis Mechanica . . . commentariis illustrata*, Parisiis, 1599. Epist. dedic. e I r; Praef. ad lect. i III v. Cf. R. Hooykaas, *Das Verhältnis von Physik und Mechanik in historischer Hinsicht*, Wiesbaden, 1963, pp. 11–16.
10. Francis Bacon, *De dignitate et augmentis scientiarum* (1623), lib. II, c. 10. *Redargutio philosophiarum* (written 1606 or 1607).
11. Bacon, *De augmentis*, II, c. 2.
12. Bacon, *Novum Organum*, I, aph. 3; Instauratio magna, distributio operis; *Novum Organum*, I, aph. 129.
13. Angelo Sala, *Anatomia vitrioli* (1617). 'Brevis demonstratio.' Cf. R. Hooykaas, *Het Begrip Element*, Utrecht, 1933, pp. 148–157.
14. Ecclesiastes 1:12–13.
15. Fr. Bacon, *The Advancement of Learning* (1605), Bk. I.
16. J. Wilkins, *The Discovery of a New World* (1638), Bk. I, prop. xiv.
17. 1 Corinthians 8:1.
18. 1 Corinthians 13:1. Fr. Bacon, *Advancement of Learning*, Bk. I.
19. James 1:17.
20. C. S. Lewis, *The Abolition of Man*, New York, 1947.

CHAPTER IV

THE RISE OF EXPERIMENTAL SCIENCE

One of the indispensable conditions for the rise of modern science was the assiduous application of the experimental method. Immediate observation of nature may be important, but in general a deliberate experiment will elicit less ambiguous answers from nature to the questions that are put to her. Scientific experimentation is not the same as technology or applied science; its first aim is not to gain power over nature but to discover its secrets by rationally planned devices.

In order to be accepted, scientific experimentation first had to receive moral sanction. That is, it had to avoid any suspicion of being used as an instrument of illicit curiosity or of lust for power. Secondly, scientific experimentation had to receive social sanction; that is, it should not be considered an unworthy pursuit for a philosopher or a free citizen. As experimentation is a kind of manual work, it goes without saying that the evaluation of the manual trades ran parallel with that of experimentation. Moreover, experimentation originally borrowed its instruments from the trades, so that the most intellectual artisans—the engineers and architects—played a large role in introducing experiments into scientific method. Accordingly the rise of modern science is to a large extent the rise of experimental science, and this is related to the religious and social evaluation of manual work and technology.

A. THE EVALUATION OF MANUAL WORK AND
EXPERIMENTATION IN ANTIQUITY

a. *Manual Trades in Antiquity*

In pre-Socratic Greece, that is, before the fourth century, manual work was highly esteemed. Solon in the sixth century required of each citizen of Athens to learn a trade and Pericles, in the fifth century, declared that artisans did not lack political sense. This latter remark reveals, however, that the opposite view had already been put forward. Lycurgus forbade the Spartans to occupy themselves with trades. Afterwards a feeling arose, in particular among the aristocrats, that manual work should be left to slaves, and that free artisans were little better than these. Leisure was indispensable for fulfilling the duties attached to the government and defence of the country. According to Herodotus, both Greeks and barbarians looked on artisans as inferior; among the Greeks the Spartans in particular held this view, whereas the Corinthians did not despise them to the same degree.

The great idealistic Athenian philosophers especially were of the opinion that the intellectual and spiritual development that was necessary for exercising the duties of the citizen could not take place in conjunction with manual work. The aristocratic feelings of these philosophers allowed an exception to be made only for military work, while their conservatism urged them to give honour to agriculture, which was considered to be close to nature and the simple life.

Plato considers agriculture to be the basis of life in his ideal state, while the manual labour connected with it should, of course, be left to slaves.[1] Xenophon, too, feels that a free citizen should not cultivate manual trades because these, and in particular those that involve the handling of fire, have an unhealthy influence on the body as well as on the mind and morality.² Men should follow the belief of the king of the Persians, who holds that husbandry and the art of warfare are the noblest and the most necessary pursuits. He pays as much attention to the one as to the other, as both are equally necessary to the support of the country. The land could not be tilled unless defended by warriors, whereas warriors could not live without the aid of the farm workers. Xenophon adds the story of the Persian prince, Cyrus, who took as much pride in cultivating and stocking land as in being a warrior. He proudly declared that he measured and arranged his 'paradise' himself, that he even did part of the planting with his own hands, and that he never sat down to eat without first working hard at some task either martial or agricultural. Such occupations as these, then, besides being traditionally acceptable, were made more acceptable still to Xenophon because a great prince had taken an interest in them. Furthermore the bodily training of agricultural work was seen to be good exercise for the free citizen and the prospective warrior.³

Aristotle, even more strongly perhaps than his immediate predecessors, emphasized the evil influences of the *banausikai technai*. He held that only the nomad, the farmer, the fisher, the hunter led really productive and natural lives, while a commercial occupation especially was to be despised. Yet, in Aristotle's ideal state, it is not primarily agriculture and warfare that should occupy the free citizen; leisure is necessary for the development of virtue and for participation in politics. In the ideal State, therefore, the citizen was not a tiller of the soil and most certainly not a follower of mechanical or mercantile trades, as these are ignoble and inimical to virtue. The warriors ought not to cultivate their own land, but leave this to slaves.[4] Contemplation, in Aristotle's opinion, is an even higher activity of the intellect than politics and warfare, for it has its purpose within itself; it exists for its own sake only and it is the activity which comes most near to the self-contemplating activity of the Prime Mover. Practical arts, on the other hand, always look for some advantage outside their own activity.[5] The free artisan is barely given a place in Aristotle's ideal State; he does the work of a slave, without having the right mental attitude of obedience, so that in fact he is inferior to a slave. The slave is, in Aristotle's conception, an 'animated tool', and if robots existed who could do all the work, slaves would become superfluous.[6] Aristotle evidently felt this to be an absurdity.

The Roman philosopher Cicero, too, thought that all artisans performed vulgar and sordid work; a mechanical workshop 'contains nothing fit for a freeborn man'[7]; retail trade is a sordid occupation, but wholesale trade should not be wholly rejected, especially not when the business man retires from the maritime town to a country seat; in that case he has some claim to esteem.

b. *Applied Science in Antiquity*

The low esteem in which manual labour was held implied a similar attitude to applied science. The learned cultivators of mathematics and theoretical mechanics considered it below their dignity to occupy themselves with the practical applications of their inventions; they left these to the artificers. Moreover, to philosophers of the Platonic school the investigation of *material* things was inferior to the pursuit of *spiritual* things. Manual work, even for a scientific end, was considered beneath the dignity of the philosopher. Plato's friends Eudoxus and Archytas were the first to put the mechanical sciences into practice. They had demonstrated by means of concrete examples and with the help of instruments some theses they could not prove in a logical way. Plato then chides them for spoiling the beauty of geometry by abandoning intellectual instruments and resorting to material means which required despicable manual work. Thus, at the moment when they could have started to combine, Plato tried to separate experimental and applied science from pure science.

Of course, 'applied science', cultivated with a practical and useful end in view, was still accorded lower status than pure science built upon experiment. Even the term geometry (*ge*, earth; *metron*, a measure) must have annoyed Plato. In his opinion, there were too many terms in that science which reminded one of manual work (e.g. plumb-line); 'their language smells of slavery'; scientists use the language of people whose purpose is practical application, whereas the true purpose of mathematics is knowledge.[8] The arithmetical study of numbers is a lofty and philosophical occupation, but calculation is vulgar and for the use of merchants and retail traders only. In the sixteenth century Peter Ramus (though a great admirer of Plato) was to point out that the following of Plato's advice on the divorce of science from its applications was one of the reasons for the stagnation of science until his own time.

Xenophon, on the other hand, more practical than Plato, had a higher appreciation of the simple applications of mathematics for measuring land and for calculating the profits of the field. He had, however, little sympathy for a disinterested science of nature, which he regarded as displeasing to the gods, who do not like men to find out how they regulate the courses of the planets.[9] At any rate, he, too, did not want any co-operation between science and technology.

Aristotle, in whose system the visible world possesses full reality, had less metaphysical prejudice against practical science than had Plato, but his social prejudice against applied science was strong. In his *Metaphysics*, he expounded the theory that for a free man, who exists only for his own sake, the sole worthy occupation is a science cultivated for its own sake. Only after the necessary technological inventions had been made could true science arise in places where people had leisure to cultivate it.[10]

c. *The Engineers in Antiquity*

Amongst the manual arts that of the architect was the most acceptable, or rather the least reprehensible, to Plato, because it involved the greatest use of mathematics. In particular he had a certain appreciation for the *mechanopoios* who constructed war machines, thereby perhaps saving a whole town. Yet, as he said to the democratic Athenians, 'you would despise him and his art'; you would not be willing to give to such a man's son your daughter nor to marry *his* daughter.[11]

Archimedes made many mechanical instruments, but only in order to defend the city that was in danger. He did not write about such vulgar things which, according to Plutarch, 'he considered low and *banausos*', and he restricted his thirst for knowledge to those things that are beautiful, without contaminating them by any application. Only in medicine was manual work really honoured by the Greeks; the Hippocratic physician was at the same time a surgeon, *cheirourgos*—a hand-worker. By the time of the Romans, however, surgery was already on a lower level. Cicero thought that scholarly jobs such as medicine, architecture and teaching, which required great intellect, were honourable occupations for those people 'to whose class they are fitting'. Posidonius was the only one who attributed the great technical inventions, such as the wheel or the art of baking bread, to scholars, although he believed that they immediately left the application of their discoveries to others. But even this went too far in the eyes of Seneca. He believed that the hammer and tongs had been invented by somebody with a lively, acute, but not deep and lofty spirit, because things like that could only be found with a bent body and a mind directed towards the earth. All technical inventions have been made by miserable slaves; wisdom has its seat higher up, it does not instruct the *hands*, but the *mind*.[12]

The engineers themselves, of course, did not acquiesce in the devastating verdicts of the philosophers. The Stoic tenet that true wisdom leads to peace of mind was jestingly applied by Hero of Alexandria (first century) to the fabrication of war machines, which put the citizens at ease, as attacks will be prevented when the enemy knows that the city is well equipped with those machines. Self-respect was also evident when the engineer Pappus energetically rejected the Platonic opinion that mathematics would suffer harm through being joined to mechanical application.

In spite of the philosophers, then, there was a fairly strong technological tradition in Hellenistic civilization. But however much mechanics may have been applied to warfare and to the making of artificial toys and other scientific diversions, their applications in civil life remained disappointingly far below the potential capacity. In the first century B.C. a Greek poet sang the praises of the newly invented waterwheel, which was to deliver the women from the hard labour of grinding corn and which seemed to announce a return to the supposedly leisurely life of the primitive Age. Nevertheless, this mechanical mill remained a rarity during the next twelve centuries. Perhaps because of the abundance of 'animated tools', both human and animal, the need for 'non-animated, self-moving instruments' was hardly felt. It was certainly no lack of technological skill which hindered the transition from theory to practice, but rather the contempt for manual labour. Science was something that belonged to the head alone and not to the hands.

d. *Experimentation in Antiquity*

Certainly many examples have survived of cleverly contrived scientific experiments; contrived, that is, with the aim of eliciting from nature an answer to some question, or of confirming an hypothesis. Yet the general impression made by ancient science is that it had been built upon speculation, and sometimes upon exact observation as in astronomy and zoology, but that experimentation played a very subordinate role. Plato had only scorn for the Pythagoreans, 'those good people, who inflict a thousand tortures on the strings and put them on the rack and wring them with their keys'.

It is perfectly clear that the Greeks could make experiments, but it is not at all clear why they made such little use of this scientific tool. One reason might be that all beginning is difficult; very often blind alleys have to be entered in order that those who come afterwards can be warned against them. Nevertheless, the founders of modern science rapidly succeeded in achieving much more with the same means.

We have already pointed out that rationalism, the deification of nature and the underestimation of art, as well as disregard for manual work, were all factors which militated against the use of experiments. Rationalism always tends to look on experimental verification of its deductions as superfluous, whereas naturalism implies that artificial activities cannot give a real insight into natural events. The analysis of natural events in the science of mechanics, which divides them into idealized parts, would have been considered a destruction of an organic process. All experimentation must have seemed to be akin to trying to study physiology on the disjoined members of a cadaver in an anatomical laboratory. People who thought along the same lines as those who held that 'if the heavens were to stand still, tow would not burn', would not have been much concerned by the impossibility of testing such verdicts by experience. In a science of mechanics in which the medium played an essential role in the explanation of motion, it must have seemed absurd to dissect natural motion so that one of the parts was ideal motion in empty space. Moreover, many experiments deal with phenomena and things which do not occur in 'nature left to herself'. According to the way of thought of the ancient world, such artificial phenomena could not give an insight into natural ones; *mechanics* had no place in *physics*. Finally, a philosopher considered it beneath his dignity to use the working methods of mechanics to solve his scientific problems, and he certainly felt no urge to put his science at the service of mechanical workers. There was a wide gap between the workers with the hand (the mechanicians) and the workers with the head (the philosophers).

B. THE JUDAEO-CHRISTIAN EVALUATION OF MANUAL WORK

a. *Manual Trades in the Bible*

When we come to consider the biblical attitude, we meet with a positive appreciation of the manual arts. Even before the Fall man had 'to dress and to keep' the garden of Eden[13]; after the Fall it was the fatigue of labour, not labour itself, which was the punishment. The biblical authors do not praise the *otium* (leisure), which according to the philosophers was a characteristic and a virtue of the life of the Greek citizen. The rule given in the Bible for the good life is that of the commandment: 'Six days thou shalt labour, and do all thy work'.[14] Consequently, the crafts were honoured as instituted by God, who gave to men the talents for exercising them;[15] who 'filled' the builders of the tabernacle 'with the spirit of God, in wisdom and in knowledge and in all manner of workmanship',[16] and who 'created the smith'.[17] Jewish rabbis had to learn a trade. Jesus was a carpenter,[18] (*tekton*), and the son of a carpenter,[19] and Paul asked the Thessalonians to work with their hands,[20] as he had given the example himself[21]; by 'his occupation he was a tentmaker' (*skenopoios*).[22]

In the Bible all labour is considered holy to the Lord; it is irrelevant whether it is performed by a slave or by a free man. Occupation with material things, which are, no less than immaterial things, God's creatures, is not thought to be dishonourable. God Himself created all visible and invisible things,[23] without any delegation of responsibility to intermediate beings.

Consequently, those factors in Greek philosophy that hampered the development of experimental science are not present in the Bible; the craftsman is honoured and therefore so too is manual work; nature is not set above human art as both have been 'created'; matter is not inferior, but a creature of God; leisure is not superior to work. The God of Israel did not retire into the way of being proper to Him, nor is He absorbed in self-contemplation. On the contrary, He is active; 'He works hitherto'[24] in a continual creation and He directs the history of mankind. Thus is given the indispensable religious sanction to action and, indirectly, to experimental science. Of course this does not imply that Israel in fact developed a technology of its own; it is quite evident that in this respect it had to borrow from the neighbouring countries.[25]

b. *Manual Trades and Experimentation in Christendom*

For the building materials of Science (logic, mathematics, the beginning of a rational interpretation of the world) we have to look to the Greeks; but the vitamins indispensable for a healthy growth came from the biblical concept of creation. The fact that the victory of Christianity did not bring an immediate liberation from the bonds of Greek metaphysics in no way disproves this statement. The compromise of Christian religion, first with Platonism, then with Aristotelianism, strongly influenced not only secular learning but also theology. Even the positive biblical appreciation of the crafts hardly overcame the traditional attitudes of Graeco-Roman (and perhaps also autochthonous) social conceptions, especially after the first force of love had spent itself and Christianity had become a firmly established world religion.

Yet in the Middle Ages technology progressed considerably. Watermills (after 1050) and, a little later, windmills were brought into the service of industry. There still were, however, great social obstacles to the introduction of technological novelties. Moreover, scholastic teaching contributed to the keeping alive of the contrast between the liberal and the illiberal or 'servile' arts, and the prejudices against the latter. As well as a moral scale of values that put the contemplative and more ascetic intellectual and religious occupations above the manual trades, there was also a feudal hierarchy in which each rank had its own duties; the nobility to defend, the clergy to pray, and the workers to keep the others alive. And even this latter hierarchy had a moral significance: according to Thomas Aquinas a king who ruled well would receive a higher reward in Heaven than a subject who lived well under such a ruler.

In spite of this attitude, scientific experiments were performed, though rarely, and even by clergymen and noblemen. Peter of Maricourt's *Letter on the Magnet* (1269) demanded of the artificer in experimental science not only a knowledge of theory but also the possession of manual skill, which would enable him to correct errors which he could never have detected with physical and mathematical knowledge alone. The Franciscan friar Roger Bacon referred to Peter of Maricourt as 'the master of experiments' who was skilful in theoretical and technical arts and cared nothing for quarrels over *words*, but occupied himself entirely with the *works* of wisdom. However, as a group, it was only the alchemists who gave an important place in their work to experiments. Instead of being ashamed of having blackened their hands with coal, they proudly styled themselves 'philosophers through fire'. To contemporary philosophers such an expression must have sounded self-contradictory; philosophy could not be built upon the work of the hands, least of all on that banausic art that handled fire.

The remarkable treatise of the emperor Frederic II, *On the Art of Hunting with Birds*, besides giving a wealth of information on the life of falcons and their prey, showed a critical and experimental spirit. But again, this approach was exceptional and not at all typical of medieval zoology. It was separated by a wide gap from scholastic zoology, which was less soberminded and was overloaded with much traditional lore on animals, uncritically abstracted from earlier works. In natural history there was an official, traditional science continuing side by side with the practical knowledge concentrated in the 'mechanical arts', which, to the modern reader, often seems much more 'scientific'. For us today the maps of the early sea-pilots are more satisfactory than those of conventional medieval geography.

As a result of this attitude medieval science has acquired a reputation for barrenness. Yet, the power of observation and the technological skill displayed in the practical works, and the acuteness of reasoning of the philosophical treatises, abundantly show that it was not lack of ability that made medieval science somewhat stagnant. Much the same points could be made in a discussion upon medieval science as upon that of ancient science.

Medieval science was too rationalistic, and even when there was an appeal to experience, this still remained the experience mentioned in books. According to Thomas Bradwardine (1338), a magnet with iron hanging on it does not weigh more than one without it, 'as experience teaches us'; and this 'experiment' was mentioned again by Heinrich von Langenstein, who evidently had not checked it. Medieval textbooks contained many thought experiments, but they were never scientifically tested and they were not even intended to be tested. Scientific demonstrations always ran 'when A and B are true', then C and D must follow. Thus, the same phenomena (one instance was that of free fall) are treated by different authors on the assumption of different hypotheses, but no effort was made to decide between alternatives as a consequence of performing an experimental test. The best one could say of this method is that it trained the mind and developed the skill of precise formulation.

Secondly, medieval philosophers, too, considered experimentation a 'mechanical' business. Even Albertus Magnus

87

(1193-1280), one of the most scientific among the philosophers, and one who had a great interest in observations and
practical affairs, deprecatingly dismissed an opponent with
the words: 'Gilgil was a mechanic and not a philosopher'.

In the Middle Ages, as in antiquity, reason led experience
into captivity, art was judged incapable of successful competition with nature, and technology was separated from
science. Head and hand were not encouraged to co-operate.

C. THE CO-OPERATION OF HEAD AND HAND IN EARLY MODERN SCIENCE

a. *Mechanical and Liberal Arts in the Sixteenth Century*

The co-operation of head and hand became much closer
during the period of the Renaissance. The emancipation of
the burghers, very often craftsmen themselves, led to a
higher value being placed on manual work as well as on
commerce and industry, except among those humanists
whose servility towards the ancients by far exceeded that
of the schoolmen. Scientists with technological interests, and
sometimes even manual skill, mixed with artificers who
wanted to give their work a scientific foundation. Gerard
Mercator in the Southern Netherlands, Nicolaus Kratzer
in Oxford, Hartmann and Schoner in Nürnberg, were
scholars with great skill in making maps, globes and sun-
dials. On the other hand, intelligent artisans and engineers,
like Albrecht Durer in Nürnberg and Simon Stevin in
Holland, sought contact with mathematicians, astronomers
and philosophers, and themselves wrote scientific books.
In commercial and industrial centres like Florence, Nürnberg and Antwerp especially, there was close co-operation
between scientists and artisans. In Nürnberg, for example,
the ironfounder Sebald Beheim, at the beginning of the

sixteenth century, asked the mathematician and clergyman Johannes Werner to translate Euclid into German for the benefit of his son. He suggested that each thesis should be accompanied by practical applications.

Luis Vives (1492–1540), who lived for many years in the Netherlands, mentioned the example of Virulus, the president of a College of Louvain in the fifteenth century, who contacted craftsmen of all kinds. Vives advised young scholars to follow this example by visiting the workshops, and to compose a 'history of the arts' which would greatly augment knowledge: an 'occupation fully worthy of the burgher'. The peasants and craftsmen, according to him, knew the nature of concrete things better than 'those great philosophers' who, instead of real nature, of which they were ignorant, imagined another consisting of 'Forms, Ideas and other chimerae'.

Paracelsus, too, advised his readers to gather knowledge from the common people. His follower, the Danish physician Peder Sörensen (1540–1608) advised young people to investigate mountains and lakes; to observe animals, plants and minerals; to make chemical experiments, and not to be ashamed to learn from peasants the secrets of earth and heaven.[26] And the humanist physician George Agricola stressed the usefulness of mining, which he regarded as a gift of God, an honest occupation for decent people, in spite of what the ancients wrote against it.

The humanist Peter Ramus (1515–1572), whose works were especially influential amongst the Puritans in England and America, was very much concerned with the relations between the liberal and the mechanical arts. He believed in a close co-operation between artificers and philosophers and advised the latter to visit the street of the bankers and merchants in Paris in order to learn the practice of reckoning.

He proudly declared that there was no mechanical work-shop in Paris that he had not thoroughly investigated more than once, and he reckoned practical applications to be more important than pure science. Ramus often referred to Socrates, always using—though he did not expressly mention the fact—quotations from the Xenophontic version of Socrates' words,[27] and he rejected Plato's 'blind prejudice' in praising contemplation and dismissing popular practical applications. In Ramus' opinion mathematical sciences had almost been destroyed by this prejudice, as they could flourish only when stimulated by the practice of the crafts-men. He put calculation above the theory of numbers, land-measuring above pure geometry, nautical science above theoretical astronomy, and in so doing he over-emphasized the usefulness of these applied sciences so much that he was nicknamed a *usuarius*.

A Cambridge Ramist, Gabriel Harvey, praised the eminence of the instrument maker Humphrey Cole, the ship-wright Matthew Baker, the architect John Shute, the gun-founder William Bourne, the nautical expert Robert Norman, and the chemist John Hester, saying that these 'empirics' would be remembered when greater scientists were forgotten. It was arrogant, he felt, to despise the skilled manual worker, 'howsoever unlectured in schools or unlettered in books he may be'. He pointed out that the great mathematicians Digges, Harriot and Dee had the greatest esteem for inventive craftsmen. Evidently not only were eminent artificers interested in science, but there were also outstanding scholars interested in technology; scientific knowledge was put to serve the mechanical arts.

This mutual interest was helped by the growing willing-ness of the scholars to divulge their learning to the un-learned, that is to those ignorant of Greek and Latin. About

1550 Robert Recorde, physician and theological writer, wrote his mathematical works in English for the benefit of craftsmen. Leonard Digges said that he did not want to hide his talents and shut up his knowledge in foreign tongues, but that he wrote in English for the benefit of people such as surveyors ('landmeters'), carpenters or bricklayers. His son Thomas Digges turned from purely contemplative mathematics to 'experimental notions'. The learned John Dee made the books of his large library available to his artificer acquaintances. From 1588 on, Thomas Hood gave public lectures on mathematics and astronomy in London for mariners, craftsmen and soldiers. In 1598 Gresham College in London was founded as a meeting place for the learned and the mechanicians, and lectures on science, mathematics and theology were delivered in Latin and in English. The famous Henry Briggs, Henry Gellibrand and Samuel Foster were amongst its professors and it is plain from their personal biographies that the college also deserved its reputation for being a hotbed of puritanism.

In the Netherlands about 1600 there was the same close co-operation between scholars and practical men. A school for engineers was established at Leyden University, where the teaching was to be in the Dutch language. The Reformed minister Peter Plancius taught nautical science to seamen from the pulpit of the Oudezyds Kapel in Amsterdam. In the beginning of the seventeenth century the learned Dr. Isaac Beeckman founded a Mechanical College in Rotterdam, whose members were Beeckman himself (assistant head-master of the Latin school), together with a silk-dyer, a merchant, a millwright, a shipwright, a carpenter, a physician, a mathematician and a surgeon. When Beeckman was Headmaster in Dordrecht he founded the first meteorological station in Europe; he made astronomical observations with the help of the Reformed minister Philips van Lansbergen, and had amongst his pupils George Ent and Jan de Witt, who became famous, the one as Harvey's supporter, the other as a statesman and mathematician.

b. *The Religious Sanction for Manual and Experimental Work*

It goes without saying that this co-operation of artificers and scholars led to a rapid development and refinement of the experimental method. Manual skill and acute methodical thinking now went together. Experimental work could become respectable once the mechanician's labour became accepted as honourable. The social emancipation of the artisan class, especially in typical burgher societies such as Nürnberg, Antwerp, London and Amsterdam, developed alongside a religious emancipation, which furthered an ethics of labour in which every calling, and not only that of a priest, was considered as 'divine'.

Undoubtedly, the general familiarity with the Bible in Reformation circles stimulated this conception. The sixteenth-century Puritan theologian William Perkins considered a manual trade, performed to the glory of God and the benefit of mankind, to be as blessed before God as that of a magistrate or a minister of religion. Hugh Latimer told his audience that nobody should disdain to follow Christ, the carpenter, in a 'common calling', as all occupations were blessed by His example. In the next century we find George Herbert, in his well-known poem *Elixir*, teaching that the clause 'For Thy sake', makes a servant's drudgery divine: 'Who sweeps a room as for Thy laws, makes that and the action fine'. The wedding service of the Netherlands' Reformed Churches speaks of the 'divine calling' of the husband. It was recognized that it was not manual work as such, but its toilsome nature, which was the penalty for sin.

Technological improvements were sometimes considered as part of a Christian restoration, precisely because they lessened the burdensome character of manual labour.

Ideas such as these certainly enhanced the self-esteem of the craftsmen. Isaac Beeckman (1588–1637) had been trained as a theologian for the ministry in the Reformed Church and he had also taken the degree of doctor of medicine. Yet he preferred for several years to follow the family trade of a chandler and a manufacturer of water conduits, because this work left him more freedom and gave him the chance to carry out physical experiments for which, at that time, mechanical workshops were much better equipped than universities. Beeckman's choice was an indication that in Holland and Zeeland a scholar did not consider it beneath his dignity to follow a trade. The Huguenot potter Bernard Palissy (sixteenth century) was another who was proud of his work as an artisan; he exhorted young noblemen to make inventions for the improvement of agriculture instead of squandering time and money in pleasure-seeking. Agriculture, so he said, was 'a right labour, worthy of being praised and honoured', and one which required more 'philosophy' (science) than any other occupation.[28]

The method used, an investigation by mechanical means, was now consistent with the subject investigated: the world mechanism. That is why experimental philosophy (a term referring to the experimental method that was applied) had to become to a large extent mechanical philosophy (a term borrowed from the theoretical conception). This identification was given theological backing by Monantheuil (1599) who called God a mechanician and the world a machine.[29] In his case, however, the strength of contemporary social prejudice against manual workers was revealed in the emphasis laid on the statement that God 'mechanises' by His word and not by His hands; mechanics was glorified not by exalting manual work, but by stressing that it need not be manual.

Francis Bacon was more radical. He maintained that although in general it was considered dishonourable for a learned man to stoop to enquire into mechanical matters, this was, nevertheless, the most fundamental way of building a natural science that did not consist of subtle speculations, but helped to relieve the burdens of life. It was wrong to think that the dignity of the human mind could be impaired by coming into contact with experiments and material things, as though it were illiberal to practise them. One should put aside prejudices against the investigation of nature with the help of mechanical arts, because such pursuits as agriculture, chemistry, glassblowing or soapmaking all changed natural things and thereby revealed their nature.[30]

Bacon recognized in 1605 that, in order to continue the scientific reformation, a reformation would be needed in the schools. He suggested that less logic and rhetoric should be taught, and that more concrete things should be dealt with; botanical and astronomical demonstrations, the use of globes and maps and chemical and mechanical experiments should be introduced into the curriculum. These proposals were not entirely new; Vives, Palissy and Recorde had all made similar remarks. The universities, however, were not yet ready to accept these new methods and their development was left to Gresham College and the learned societies.

c. *The Puritan Attitude towards Experimental Science*

Among the Puritans especially, Bacon's ideas on the reformation of learning met with a warm approval. Comenius' visit to England (1640–1641) was intended to support reforms in the Baconian spirit.[31] We find Cromwell's army

chaplain John Webster demanding the provision of labora-
tories in the universities as well as libraries, so that young
people would not be trained entirely in empty speculations,
but might learn to use their hands and to become accustomed to labour, 'and that they put their fingers in the oven,
so that they get familiar with the wonders of chemistry'.
Moreover, the hard reality of experimental facts would
prevent them from 'growing proud with the brood of their
own brains'.[32] William Petty, a cloth-dyer who became a
physician and, during Cromwell's reign, a professor of
anatomy in Oxford, wanted even children of the upper
class to learn a craft, so that they would be taught to make
experiments and might become in their turn protectors of
science. Thus there was a general desire for more 'ocular
demonstrations', more experiments 'with the hands', more
chemistry, and a 'multiplication of mechanical knowledge'.

John Wilkins (who was to become Cromwell's brother-
in-law) was critical of the Greeks for their contempt of the
practical arts. It is characteristic of the practical attitude of
Wilkins that he regarded Galileo primarily as a successor of
the engineers and not of the philosophers of Antiquity. This
attitude meant a total reversal of the order in which the
scholars of their own time appreciated the men in these
categories of human activity.

Wilkins was the leading spirit of the group that was to
become the Royal Society after the Restoration. Though
people of all political and ecclesiastical parties worked together there, the majority of the founders had Puritan
leanings.[33] In this society, as Sprat said, 'the tradesman, the
merchant, the scholar' represented the 'union of Men's
hands and Reasons'; they preferred 'works before words',
and they used the language of artificers and merchants, and
not that of philosophers. In Sprat's opinion 'philosophy will

then attain to perfection, when either the Mechanic labourers shall have philosophical heads, or the Philosophers shall have mechanical hands'.[34]

A clear testimony to the growth of intellectual change in that period was given by John Wallis, who before the Puritan Revolution stated that mathematical studies were hardly looked upon as academic, whereas in 1670 he could say that 'the study of chemistry is not misbecoming a gentleman'. This change from neglect of the mathematical *liberal* arts (which were held in esteem even by the ancient philosophers) to approval of the most banausic of the *mechanical* arts, demonstrates that during the Puritan period a movement that was already in existence had made great progress. More and more the learned men of Northern and Western Europe had realized that for natural science to prosper it was not sufficient to think with their heads, but that, as the Puritan clergyman Nathanael Carpenter put it, they ought also to have 'their wits in their hands'.

NOTES TO CHAPTER IV

1. Plato, *Laws* V, 743 D; vii, 806 D.
2. Xenophon, *Oeconomicus*, iv, 2–3.
3. Xenophon, *Oeconomicus*, iv, 45; 12; 15; 17; 22–24, V, 1; 14.
4. Aristotle, *Politics*, vii, 9 (1, 5, 9); 8 (2–3).
5. Aristotle, *Nicomachean Ethics* X, 8; 7.
6. Aristotle, *Politics*, i, 5 (3–10); i, 2 (4, 5).
7. Cicero, *De officiis*, i, 42.
8. Plato, *Republic*, vii, 527 A–B.
9. Xenophon, *Memorabilia*, iv, 7, 2–8.
10. Aristotle, *Metaphysics*, i, 1.
11. Plato, *Gorgias*, 511 D—512 D.
12. Seneca, *Epist. mor.*, 90, 26.
13. Genesis 2:5.
14. Deuteronomy 5:13.
15. Exodus 35:35.

16. Exodus 31:3.
17. Isaiah 54:16.
18. Matthew 6:3.
19. Matthew 13:55.
20. 1 Thessalonians 4:11.
21. 2 Thessalonians 3:8–11.
22. Acts 18:3.
23. John 1:3; *Confess. Nic.*
24. John 5:17.
25. 1 Chronicles 14:1; 2 Chron. 2:14.
26. P. Severinus, *Ideae Medicinae philosophicae*, 1571.
27. For Ramus' attitude towards the manual arts, cf R. Hooykaas, *Humanisme, science et réforme—Pierre de la Ramée.* Leyden, 1958, especially ch. VIII D: 'Les deux Socrate', pp. 59–62.
28. B. Palissy, *Récepte véritable* (1563), Au lecteur.
29. H. Monantholius, *Aristotelis Mechanica . . .*, Parisiis, 1599. Epistola dedicatoria, a III r.
30. Fr. Bacon, *Novum Organum*, I, aph. 83; *De augmentis*, II, c. 2; *Parasceve*, aph. 5.
31. J. A. Comenius, *Via Lucis* (written 1641); preface (publ. 1668).
32. John Webster, *Academiarum Examen*, London, 1651, p. 106.
33. It is only by narrowing down the notion of 'puritan' in conformity with personal preconceptions that this could be denied. The fact that Sprat, in his defence of the Royal Society, stressed the conformity of the New Philosophy with the Church of England and denied any connection with Puritanism, does not prove anything against it. Sprat, who was a trimmer himself, would have acted unwisely, if he had not emphasized the Reformed character of the Church of England while depicting at the same time—as was the fashion of the day—as typically 'puritan' the radicals and 'enthusiasts'. In this way, his own past (and that of men like Wilkins) would no longer be 'puritan'.
34. Th. Sprat, *The History of the Royal Society of London*, 4th ed., London, 1734, p. 434.

CHAPTER V

SCIENCE AND THE REFORMATION

A. REFORMATION INFLUENCE ON SCIENCE

a. *The Protestants' Share in Scientific Activity*

Sociological research has established that, until quite recently, Protestants have been relatively more numerous among scientists than one would expect from their total number. A. de Candolle (1885) found that among the foreign members of the Académie des Sciences in Paris, from 1666 to 1883, the Protestants by far outnumbered the Roman Catholics. In the population of Western Europe outside France the proportion of Roman Catholics to Protestants was as six to four, whereas among the foreign members of the Académie des Sciences the proportion was as six to twenty-seven. In Switzerland the numbers of Roman Catholics and Protestants were as two to three, and during the period mentioned there were fourteen Swiss Protestant members of the Académie and no Roman Catholics.[1] Prof. J. Pelseneer, the Belgian historian of science, found that in the Southern Netherlands (Belgium) in the sixteenth century the Protestants formed but a small minority (perhaps 100,000 people), yet Protestant scientists were far more numerous than those of the Roman Catholic faith.[2] The American sociologist, Professor R. K. Merton, pointed out in 1938 that among the group of ten scientists who during the Commonwealth formed the nucleus of the body that was to become the Royal Society, seven were strongly Puritan. Sixty-two per cent of the members of the Royal Society in 1663 were clearly Puritan by origin, a percentage that is the more striking because the Puritans constituted a minority of the population.[3] Roman Catholic sociologists have confirmed that until quite recently there was a greater tendency on the part of Protestant scholars to turn to scientific and technological studies than there was among the Roman Catholics.[4, 5]

Now the growth of the exact sciences and of technology in the late sixteenth and the seventeenth centuries in Protestant circles may partly be attributed to the expansion of trade, industry and navigation; but this does not explain why there was also at the same time a great interest in botany and zoology, which were not subjects of immediate economic utility. The majority of sixteenth-century botanists belonged to the Protestant minority. Brunfels, who died in 1534, Bock (1498–1554) and Fuchs (1501–1566) were zealous Protestants[6]; so also were the great botanists of the Netherlands, Clusius (1526–1609) and Lobelius (1538–1616), and those of Switzerland, for example, Conrad Gesner (1516–1565), the friend of Zwingli and Bullinger.[6a] William Turner (1508–1568), 'the true pioneer of natural history in England'[7], played a considerable part in the introduction of Calvinism to England; he worked in direct contact with Latimer, John a Lasco and Cranmer.

The coincidence of the 'new learning' and the 'new doctrine', then, is a fact, though it is not easy to give its explanation. Several questions arise: one might ask whether religious or economic and social factors have been decisive in the evaluation of technology and experimental science. Had Reformed (or even Puritan) theology a stimulating effect on the new science, or was the social and economic development the cause of the scientific as well as the religious reformation? It is almost impossible to choose between these alternatives, as these various factors are so closely interwoven. In maritime cities, like Antwerp or London, and industrial and commercial centres, like Nürnberg, life was dynamic and less provincial than in most university towns.[8] When the university of Portugal was transferred from Lisbon to Coimbra in 1537 the move was applauded as an escape from the distraction provided by a commercial and maritime centre. On the other hand, in his inaugural address at Gresham College in 1657, Christopher Wren congratulated the city of London for its 'general relish of mathematicks and the *libera philosophia* in such a measure, as is hardly to be found in the academies themselves'.[9] In such towns as London there was a lively intercourse with other civilizations, with other religions, philosophies and customs. There was *movement* in every respect, and it is understandable that these cities, which had achieved political emancipation, were open to cultural and religious emancipation as well. New scientific ideas were easily accepted by those who were sufficiently ready to accept change of any kind. Moreover, in commercial cities religious tolerance was furthered by the interests of trade, so that we find that repression of Protestantism in sixteenth century Venice and Antwerp was rather weak and sporadic, and that in seventeenth-century Amsterdam tolerance towards Jews and Christian sects (even Socinians) was greater than in most parts of the Republic of the Seven United Provinces.

In the Scandinavian countries, however, where the whole population followed the prince and accepted the Reformation, such a selective effect could hardly have existed. For these countries, and also for the second and third generations of Protestants in countries like the Netherlands, the problem was different, for when Protestantism became an established power, adherence to the Reformed creed was in itself no possible indication of spiritual independence or progressiveness. The question that here arises is whether established Protestantism formed a hostile, a neutral or a stimulating spiritual background to the development of science and technology.

Of course other factors besides religion played a role. One contemporary author, Peter Ramus (1515–1572), attributed the revival of interest in the so-called exact sciences in Basle to the Reformation; but for some towns in Germany he put it down to economic causes, that is to the interest taken by the rulers in the mining industry[10] and to their need for military engineers. Differing social structures and conceptions also played a significant role, and it should be pointed out that the attitude of the nobility and the clergy towards trade and technology was not everywhere the same. At any rate, as noted above (pp. 75; 92), for an age in which religious sanction was necessary for something to become socially acceptable, it made a great difference whether science was distrusted, merely tolerated, or positively encouraged by the prevalent religion.

b. *Intramundane Asceticism and Scientific Activity*

What was there then in the dogmatics and ethics of the Reformed Churches that could explain their members' predilection for science? Professor Merton, under the inspiration of Max Weber's famous *Religions-soziologie*, has suggested the importance of the calvinistic doctrine of election. In Weber's opinion, a special form of the doctrine of election, stemming from the belief that performance of 'good works' is a sign of election (*Bewährungsglauben*), determined the attitude of 'this-worldly' asceticism (*innerweltliche Askese*) taken up by the Reformed, the Puritans included. From this asceticism ensued a great economic activity, so that, perhaps unwillingly and unconsciously, a religious attitude came to foster modern capitalism.[11] Merton extended this thesis by demonstrating that this attitude of self restraint, simplicity and diligence also furthered interest in and aptitude for scientific and technological research.[12]

Weber and Merton, however, made it plain by their own investigations that 'innerworldly' asceticism was also a characteristic of Quakers, Independents, Mennonites and Pietists, groups which, as Weber himself pointed out, were not wholly predestinarian and thus could not feel the need for election to be confirmed through the manifestation of good works.[13] Though the common factor in the tenets of the predestinarians and of the non-predestinarians, the injunction to intramundane asceticism, may have exerted a wide influence, no factual proof has been given that in the case of the Calvinists the doctrine of predestination and election has anything to do with their scientific activities. Merton was on rather shaky ground when he relied on the views of Richard Baxter, who considered only the glory of God and the benefit of mankind when he dealt with the subject of scientific research.[14] The attitude of the Calvinists in this matter was apparently somewhat general; a certain ethical conception of the human task on earth, rather than any special dogma, would seem to have been their main incentive or justification for the study of science.

C. E. Raven has claimed that Calvin's 'stress upon election and the extremes to which this led his followers did not favour scientific studies or any deep concern with the world of nature'. According to Merton, however, 'the fact that Calvin himself deprecated science only enhances the paradox that from him stemmed a vigorous movement which furthered interest in this very field'. This remark is only one of many rash statements about the relation of theological and scientific tenets, especially of those made with regard to Calvin.

Whereas Merton derived from Calvin's doctrine of election a theory suggesting a preference for science among his followers, Raven attributed the opposite effect to the same cause. In both sociological and theological attempts to relate Calvinism and Puritanism with capitalism, or with science and technology, one all too often finds seemingly logical or plausible deductions drawn from premises which themselves are weak. These interpretations are then advanced as facts, sometimes even without concern for concrete proofs. Thus, Raven's quite sympathetic accounts of William Turner and John Ray (two biologists of the sixteenth and seventeenth centuries respectively), contradict his own verdict cited above. Turner was a rigorous Puritan 'avant la lettre', while Ray allowed himself to be deprived of his living after the Restoration, rather than disavow his former religious allegiance. In the same way the doctrine of predestination and election has been considered both as the cause of fatalism and antinomianism and as the basis of a "Romish" concern for good works; both as a source of inactivity and of a feverish activism. Jansenism, too, with its emphasis on the doctrine of election, has had the same contradictory statements made about it. According to Merton, Jansenius' teaching turned Pascal away from the study of science; whereas in the opinion of S. F. Mason, the doctrine of election made the Jansenists science-minded.[15]

It should be recognized, however, that it was almost inevitable that a thriving and church-going burgher class should have sought for religious sanction *a posteriori* for their growing wealth. It has been pointed out that, with the growth of trade and the triumph of Independent individualism, the view came to the fore that all personal success was a sign of God's favour. The Netherlands' Pensionary Jacob Cats (1577–1660), who was a successful business man and an extremely popular poet, recommended charitable works as 'the safest deposit, since the Bank of Heaven is never reduced to bankruptcy'. There was nothing particularly Calvinistic about Cats' theology nor about the beliefs of the Anglican clergyman and mathematician Isaac Barrow, who wrote that 'exercising bounty is the most advantageous method of improving and increasing an estate'.[16] If the argument for the connection between the doctrine of election and economic activity was weak, the same may certainly be said of its allegedly close relation with technological and scientific activity.

The widely accepted 'confessions of faith' of Reformed communities are presumably the most representative documents of the prevailing opinion among genuine Calvinists of the sixteenth century. From these it would seem that in the Reformed faith good works were considered to be a 'fruit of gratitude' for salvation received, not a reassurance of having received it. According to the Heidelberg Catechism, faith has been wrought in the hearts of men by the Holy Ghost.[17] The Netherlands' Confession (the so-called 'XXXVII Articles') states that this faith takes away the terror of God; without it 'man would never do anything for the *love* of God, but only for the love of oneself and for fear of perdition'; if we had to trust in our good works, we would always be *uncertain*, 'our poor consciences would always be *tortured* if we did not put our trust in the passion and death of our Saviour'. 'The sins by which even our good works are tainted, would take away our certainty.'[18] These are not the words of tortured souls, but of those that have achieved liberation.

Consequently, the activism of members of the Reformed churches, including their taste for science, did not bear such a restless character as one might expect from reading Tawney, von Martin and some other social historians. Frequently, too, it has been overlooked that the doctrine of predestination is not specifically Calvinist, having been expounded by Saint Paul, Thomas Aquinas and Luther as well. Certainly Calvin gave the doctrine a special character but the clever constructions of sociologists fail to prove any link between his idea of predestination and either capitalism or modern science.

What strikes one most about the early Protestant scientists is their love for nature, in which they recognize the work of God's hands, and their pleasure in investigating natural phenomena. One of the fathers of comparative anatomy, the Netherlander Volcker Coiter (1534–1576), never tired of praising the Creator's providence as demonstrated in the wonderful adaptation of animal structure[19]; the botanist Clusius declared that botanical discoveries gave him as much joy as if he had found a prodigious treasure[20]; the Huguenot potter Bernard Palissy (1510–1590) passionately loved plants, 'even the most despised'. On one occasion, he became angry about the maltreatment of trees by some workmen; in his deep sympathy with these fellow-creatures he wondered why the shrubs did not cry out at the tortures they underwent at the hands of men.[21]

c. *To the Glory of God*

The central theme of Reformed theology was 'the glory of God'. Kepler wrote in 1598 that the astronomers, as priests of God to the book of nature, ought to keep in their minds not the glory of their own intellect, but the glory of God above everything else.[22] The Netherlands' Confession emphasizes that nature is 'before our eyes as a beautiful book, in which all created things, large or small, are as letters showing the invisible things of God'. The same conception of the Two Books and their parallelism is found in the work of Francis Bacon.[23]

The Reformed church taught that the duty of glorifying God for all His works should be performed by all the faculties of man, not only by the eyes, but also by the intellect. Calvin expressed the view that those who neglected the study of nature were as guilty as those who, when investigating God's works, forgot the Creator. He sharply reproved those 'phantastic' opponents of science, who said that this study only made men proud, and who did not recognize that it led to 'knowledge of God and the conduct of life'.[24] Again and again he testified to his positive appreciation of scientific research as something which penetrated deeper into the wonders of nature than did mere contemplation. When he said this he was not referring to the speculative 'physics' of his time, but to the solid empirical disciplines of that epoch: to astronomy and anatomy which revealed, as he said, the secrets of the macrocosm and the microcosm.[25]

This duty of scientific investigation was not regarded as an oppressive law, but rather was enjoyed as a duty of love and gratitude, as is evident for instance from the works of Robert Recorde (1550), Leonhard Fuchs. Thomas Digges, Bernard Palissy and Johannes Kepler. They considered scientific research in the light of the parable of the talents, which played an important role in their ethics. According to Calvin 'those who have the leisure and the ability'[26] ought not to neglect the study of astronomy. Palissy held that, as God had given him the talent to *see* things, he ought not to neglect the study of fossils, which he found when looking for clay for his workshop. The quotation: 'According to one's talents' caused Kepler to argue that the unlearned man, who praised God for what he saw with his eyes, paid Him no less honour than did the astronomer to whom God has given in addition the eye of Reason to see more clearly (1609).[27]

d. *Predestination and Determinism*

Some writers on the history of science have adduced yet another effect of the doctrine of predestination on science. They state that the Calvinist system contains a belief in immutable law, which it has in common with the system of natural science; thus the doctrine of God's foreknowledge is held to have strengthened the belief in natural law.[28] This argument seems to rest on a serious misunderstanding, as it more or less identifies predestination with determinism. Certainly the two theories have in common the implication that nothing happens by chance; but whereas the one is concerned with God's free will and implies that God, who is beyond time, has foreknowledge of what He wills, the other is a form of necessitarianism; the former stresses the reign of Jahveh, the latter that of fate and necessity.[29] The biblical authors hold that there is order in the created world, and this point is also stressed by Aquinas and the Platonist philosopher William of Conches. The last two, however, emphasize that this is a rational order, implying an element of necessity. With the Bible, on the other hand, this order bears no necessitarian character; it is not even a natural law, but a sign of God's loving care for His creatures.[30] Calvin did not deal with this order under the heading 'Predestination' (which concerned salvation), but under that of 'Providence' (which dealt rather with things of this world). It was not Calvinism but Thomism (as in the work of the Anglican divine Richard Hooker) that came close to scientific determinism[31]; whereas Calvin's standpoint on this issue had more affinity with Scotism and the moderate nominalism of Nicole Oresme[32].

In point of fact Determinism is not such a boon for science as has often been assumed. In spite of all deductions to the contrary, historical reality has shown that voluntarism and not determinism was in the long run more favourable to opening up new ways in Science. In this voluntaristic way of thinking, the order of nature was not *our* logical order, but that *willed* by God.[33] Thus if the doctrine of predestination is said to have been favourable to science, it must have been so in a way precisely the reverse of that propounded by Merton. In Calvin's *Institutes* he states in the chapter on Providence that God's fatherly hand is in all things that happen; the stars could do no harm, all fear is groundless, for God reigns. The order comes from God, but the deviations from this order, the *extra*-ordinary events, are likewise from him. From this point of view there is no essential difference between ordinary events, such as the sequence of day and night; extraordinary events, such as earthquakes; and miraculous, or even unique, events—'Sun, stand thou still'. In Calvin's writings there is no talk about super-natural acts or interventions; God's Providence is 'obscured' by those who connect it with special acts only.[34]

The result, as in the case of the nominalists, was paradoxical: the *order* too was miraculous. Isaac Beeckman (a predestinarian himself), maintained that God's Providence makes all events in nature coincide with the resolutions of His free will; the more men regulate events according to mechanical laws, the more it is possible to realize how mysterious are these events, or as Beeckman put it: 'The better we understand God's government, the more glorious and wonderful it is'. Thus, 'in science we must always proceed from wonder to non-wonder . . . but in theology we must proceed from non-wonder to wonder . . . until everything appears to be miraculous'.[35] However much, then, Calvinism might have emphasized the orderliness of the universe, this emphasis had no connection with the doctrine of predestination in its specifically Calvinist form. By and by, however, the genuine doctrine of predestination gave way to determinism and deism, and the methodological principle of causality passed from science into theology.

e. *The General Priesthood of Believers*

From the above it would appear that if the German Roman Catholic sociologist Müller-Armack was right when he said that 'nowhere, (so much) as in Protestantism, did the dogmatic structure itself work actively in the direction of the new'[36], this was not true specifically on account of the doctrine of predestination. It would seem rather that the preponderant influence might be the typically Protestant (perhaps even 'Reformed') emphasis on the 'general priesthood of all believers.' This implied the right, and even the duty, for those who had the talents, to study Scripture without depending on the authority of tradition and hierarchy, together with the right and the duty to study the other book written by God, the book of nature, without regard to the authority of the fathers of natural philosophy. The Huguenot Palissy was derided because he, a man 'without letters' (that is, ignorant of Greek and Latin), had dared to contradict the view of the ancients, who held that minerals grow like plants. A scholar, introduced under the name of 'Theorique', asks him in which book he has read his new opinion, and he retorts that he got his knowledge through the anatomy of nature and not by reading books: 'I have had no other book but heaven and earth, which is known to everybody, and it has been given to *everyman* to know and to read this beautiful book'.[37]

This sense of a general priesthood of believers encouraged Reformed laymen freely to criticize the old priests—(Palissy accused the clergy of his town of neglecting their duty to preach the gospel, and of fleecing their sheep instead of looking after them)—as well as the new presbyters: Isaac Beeckman, as a 'lay' elder of the Reformed church of Rotterdam, by his opposition to the church policy of the local ministers, showed himself no less independent in theological matters than in his scientific thinking.[38] The belief that everyone should read the book of nature according to his capacities encouraged the protagonists of the new science to urge the unlearned to help them in collecting data for the construction of a more complete natural history and geography, by communicating observations on birds and flowers, on ebb and flood, on celestial phenomena and the weather, and on the inclination of the magnetic needle.[39] Of course, this 'general priesthood' to the book of nature was not discovered by means of its theological parallel only. As we noted earlier the simple fact that navigators and artisans had put to shame the theories of the learned had also helped to lay its foundation. But the opposition of this new empirical science to the established natural philosophy strongly appealed to the Protestants. Their minds had been trained to the idea that each man accepts the responsibility for finding the truth as far as possible for himself, and that there ought to be freedom from human authority in order that the submission to divine authority may be the more complete.

Yet traditionalism remained strong in Protestant circles too. In the universities in particular conservatism and conformism reigned. As soon as a church has become 'established', a tendency to clericalism and intolerance will grow, and this explains the protests of Independents and other radicals against Presbyterianism ('new *presbyter*, old *priest* writ large'). Such clericalism was among the inconsistencies of established Protestant churches and it elicited violent reactions, especially in the Reformed churches, from Independent and radical factions and sects. Nevertheless, though the force of tradition within Protestantism was considerable, it had no official status as it was not recognized as a source of revelation. In Protestantism, moreover, there was no strong central authority similar to the Holy Office or to the Congregation of the Index. Hence individual opinion had a better chance of making itself heard, especially in countries where religious sects were many, and sometimes influential, as in Holland and England (and, for a short time, in Poland). In such lands philosophical and scientific sectarianism could easily develop and a large measure of scientific freedom was the inevitable consequence. Wilkins, writing on the University of Oxford during the Commonwealth, said that 'there is not to be wished a more general liberty in point of judgment or debate than what is here allowed'. According to him there was scarcely any consistent hypothesis, ancient or modern, for example the atomic theory and the Copernican doctrine, without its strenuous champions in that university, and there was full liberty either to agree with Aristotle or to declare against him, all 'being ready to follow the Banner of Truth by whomsoever it shall be lifted up'.

Scientists in Protestant countries were not forced to recognize non-scientists as judges in matters of science. When, in the Netherlands, the great theologian Gijsbert Voet (1588–1676) maintained the Aristotelian philosophy as an indispensable support of orthodox theology, his no less orthodox opponents of the Cocceian party either separated theology from philosophy or showed an inclination to Cartesianism. When Voet advocated the geocentric world system as the only one compatible with Holy Scripture, his influence was counterbalanced by other Reformed theologians, who preferred, or even propagated, Copernicanism, without any intervention from synods or church consistories.

As the religious Reformation assumed a free attitude not only towards medieval scholasticism but even (though more respectfully) towards the Fathers of the Church, so the scientific reformation rejected not only scholastic physics, but in many cases also the humanistic belief in the infallibility of the ancients. The English Puritan Nathanael Carpenter admitted that Lactantius was 'a pious eloquent Father', but 'the childishnesse of his arguments will . . . discover his ignorance in the very first rudiments of Cosmographie'.⁴¹

A return to the sources was urged: to the Book of Scripture in one case, to the book of nature (older even than the ancients) in the other. Criticism, not only of the scholastics, but also of the ancients, was necessary in order to assert the value of the present age. Perhaps such a free attitude was more difficult to assume for the scholars than for the unlearned, as the former knew how much the current reliable knowledge in, for instance, astronomy, mathematics and engineering, was due to the ancient heritage. Nevertheless, even the humanist Peter Ramus recognized that one single experience of an unlearned man had more weight than the authority of all the ancients; 'the true and ancient philosophy has been not lightly to believe anything from any philosopher however great he may be'.⁴²

The scientists often showed themselves more essentially Protestant than the theologians. Kepler was a devoted Lutheran, but Luther's authority did not move him to accept the Lutheran interpretation of the eucharist as the only possible or admissible one. This same freedom he maintained in scientific questions: 'Holy Lactantius, who denied that the earth is spherical; holy Augustine, who acknowledged the sphericity of the earth but rejected the existence of antipodes; holy the Officium that recognized the antipodes but rejects the motion of the earth . . . but holier yet to me is Truth, which reveals that the earth is a small sphere, that antipodes exist, and that the earth is moving'.[43] Nathanael Carpenter set his 'Free Science' (1622) against 'the superstitious cult of Aristotle' and he ended his plea for freedom of scientific research with the triumphant exclamation: 'I am free, I am bound to nobody's word except to those inspired by God'. The puritan divine John Wilkins, too, was a bold opponent of authoritarianism in science. In his opinion man ought to go in theology to the most ancient writers (the Bible), but in those sciences that increase by new experiments and discoveries, *we* are the most ancient: antiquity was the youth of the world. These arguments were to be found again in Pascal's polemics with the Jesuits some years later. According to Wilkins science is 'made up of nothing else' than novelties; in science 'truth is the daughter of time' (an expression borrowed from Bacon). Yet Wilkins did not want to press his opinion, as 'the Reader may use his own liberty' in considering whether the arguments were convincing. The multitude of authorities should not weigh most heavily, nor should 'their skill in some things make them of credit in every thing'.[44] This last thrust was to silence philosophers and theologians who used their authority to get their verdicts on scientific matters accepted.

The defenders of the New Philosophy were perfectly conscious of the analogy between the liberation from ecclesiastical and philosophical tradition by the Reformation and the liberation of science from ancient authority by the new learning. Thomas Culpeper (1655) wrote that the one did not want a pope in religion, the other rejected the 'pope in philosophy' (Aristotle), and both were collegiate in character—synods on the one hand and scientific societies on the other.[45] Thomas Sprat (1667) pointed to what the Reformation and the New Learning had in common, both 'passing by the corrupt copies, and referring themselves to the perfect originals for their instruction; the one to the Scripture, the other to the large volumes of the creatures'.[46]

B. SCIENCE AND BIBLE EXEGESIS

a. *The Bible as a Source for Science*

Quite apart from the question as to whether the general climate created by a biblical religion has been favourable to the cultivation of science, there is the problem whether the world picture contained in some biblical passages, combined with the injunction to accept the Bible as an indisputable divine authority, was not an impediment to the freedom of science. The debates that centred on the Copernican system clearly demonstrated that the non-literal or literal interpretation of certain texts decided whether the motion of the earth was admissible or not.

The issue was not whether Scripture was *wholly* or *partly* divinely inspired, for all agreed that it was, from Genesis to Revelation, the word of God. But at the same time, it was recognized that the Bible had not fallen from heaven but had been written by men, each of them using his own idiom, images, metaphors and beliefs, thus conveying eternal truth in earthen vessels. The question, then, was how far the biblical passages at issue were really authoritative divine revelation, and how far just human conceptions and ways of speech, timebound and rather irrelevant to the message of salvation and the conduct of life. Further, did the 'human' character of Scripture imply that the naive, or even errone- ous, beliefs of the writers (beliefs not conformable to 'objective', scientific, truth), had entered into the sacred text?

It is often said that Protestantism, because of its rejection of Tradition as a source of revelation, clung, even more than Roman Catholicism, to a literalistic interpretation of the Bible. This sounds plausible enough, but, as has been so often the case with historical deductions, it is not borne out by the facts.[1] This becomes evident from the answer of one of the greatest theologians of the Counter-reformation, Cardinal Robert Bellarmine, S.J. (1615), to the Carmelite Foscarini, who (like Galileo)[2] held that the theory of the motion of the earth, as it did not affect an article of faith or concern salvation, might be true, even though it was contradictory to the letter of Scripture. Bellarmine retorted that the Council of Trent had demanded that Scripture should be explained in conformity with the teaching of the Holy Fathers, and they, as well as the modern commentators on Genesis, Psalms, Ecclesiastes and Joshua, took the movement of the sun around the earth to be in the *literal* sense. The church, then, could not support an exegesis of Scripture in a sense contrary to that of the Fathers. Bellarmine rejected the objection that this subject was not a matter of faith (materia di fede *ex parte objecti*). It is a matter of faith, he claims, because of Him who is speaking (é materia di fede *ex parte dicentis*). The man who denies that Abraham had two sons, or Jacob twelve sons, is as heretical as he who denies that Christ was born from a virgin, for both statements have been made by the Holy Ghost through the mouths of the prophets and apostles. Moreover Solomon, who wrote that the sun rises and reverts to his place, was most learned in all human wisdom and had received this wisdom from God, so that it is impossible that he could affirm anything contrary to a demonstrated or demonstrable truth.[3] Here, then, Tradition as a source of revelation became an extra obstacle to the freedom of science, and all the more so as Tradition implied the influence of Greek philosophy on the interpretation of the Bible.

The diametrically opposite standpoint, which also made use of a reference to Solomon, was taken by the Puritan theologian John Wilkins, who, influenced by Calvin, wrote: 'It were happy for us, if we could exempt Scripture from Philosophical controversies: If we could be content to let it be perfect for that end unto which it was intended, for a Rule of our Faith and Obedience, and not stretch it also to be a Judge of such Natural Truths as are to be found out by our own Industry and Experience'. The Holy Ghost could easily have given us information on the latter, yet 'He has left this Travel to the sons of men to be exercised therewith'.[4] This means that Wilkins and others like him had discarded the Bible not as a directive for scientific research, but only as a source of factual information for it.

There was, of course, the temptation, especially for those who wanted to substitute a purely biblical theology for a theology based on Aristotelian principles, to found science too on a biblical instead of an Aristotelian basis. And this biblical foundation often meant that not only a general evaluation of the world was sought in the Bible but also concrete data about its structure. The so-called Mosaic philosophy (cosmology, physics, chemistry) was grounded upon biblical texts and set up against the 'heathenish philosophy' of Aristotle. The Mosaic philosophy was, however, largely a projection into Scripture of allegedly Egyptian wisdom said to derive from Abraham, or even from Seth, although, in fact, it had been gathered from late antiquity.[5]

However, the idea of setting up a 'biblical' natural science found no general acceptance among the adherents of the Reformation. The idea was rejected by such influential writers as Ramus and Francis Bacon, Kepler and Wilkins. In Bacon's opinion, to seek 'heaven and earth' in the word of God was to search for temporary things amongst the eternal; to seek philosophy in divinity was to look for the dead amongst the living.[6] In general, the 'biblicism' of the Reformed Christians was not concerned with scientific topics, and in seeking the data of science solely in the book of *creation*, they followed the example of one of their main teachers, John Calvin.[7]

b. *Calvin on Science and Scripture*

Calvin, though very critical of pagan thinking, did not repudiate everything that originated with the heathen. His doctrine of 'common grace' prevented any wholesale disavowal of the literary and scholarly heritage of the Greeks. He was too realistic and too accomplished a humanist to hold that the Fall had led to a total depravity of man in the scientific field. In Calvin's opinion, the light of truth shines clearly in the heathen, and 'if we hold the Spirit of God to be the only source of truth, we will neither reject nor despise the truth, wherever it may reveal itself, lest we offend the Spirit of God.'[8]

One might perhaps expect, then, that Calvin would follow the common practice of reading Greek cosmology into Scripture. On the contrary, however, he recognized more clearly than his contemporaries that there was a discrepancy between the Aristotelian astronomy of his days and the world picture of the Book of Genesis. Whereas Moses spoke of *one* expanse, the astronomers made a distinction between several spheres. He pointed out that Genesis calls the sun and the moon the 'great lights', whereas the astronomers prove by conclusive reasoning that the little star of Saturn is greater than the moon.[9] On the other hand Calvin did not reject the current astronomical system. As a layman in astronomy, he took for granted the system of the world that had been generally accepted since antiquity. The cause of the difference between Moses and the astronomers was, in his opinion, that Moses wrote in a popular way and described what all ordinary people, endowed with common sense, are able to follow, whereas the astronomers investigate whatever the sagacity of the human mind can understand.[10]

Thus Calvin's exegetical method was based on the Reformation doctrine which held that the religious message of the Bible is accessible to everybody. The Spirit of God, as he put it, has opened a common school for all, and has therefore chosen subjects intelligible to all. Moses was ordained a teacher of the unlearned as well as of the learned; had he spoken of things generally unknown, the uneducated might have pleaded in excuse that such subjects were beyond their capacity; therefore, Moses 'rather adapted his writing to common usage'. The Bible, then, was 'a book for laymen'; 'he who would learn astronomy and other recondite arts, let him go elsewhere'.[11]

Calvin even considered that the Holy Spirit had occasionally accommodated Himself to a vulgar error in order to bring out the meaning of His spiritual message. Commenting on Psalm 58: 4, 5 ('They are like the deaf adder that stoppeth her ear; which will not hearken to the voice of the charmers, charming never so wisely'), Calvin has doubts about the possibility of charmers charming serpents and of adders stopping their ears. He therefore suggests an alternative to the realistic interpretation: 'David borrowed the similitude out of the common error, as if he had said, there is no wiliness to be found in serpents which reigns not in these men; yea, though it be so that adders be fenced by their own slyness against enchantments, yet are these men as crafty as they'.[12]

Calvin's sound common sense is also evident when he interprets the 'waters above the heaven' of Genesis 1 as clouds. They are neither a real ocean, as the literalists thought, nor angels, as the allegorical exegetes (such as Origen) would have it: 'For it appears opposed to common sense, and quite incredible, that there should be certain waters above the heaven'. Calvin preferred to think of these waters as 'such as the rude and unlearned also may perceive'.[13] He did not believe that the authority of Scripture demands acceptance of unreasonable tenets regarding nature: 'the assertion of some, that they embrace by faith what they have read here concerning the waters above the heavens notwithstanding their ignorance respecting them, is not in accordance with the design of Moses'.[14]

All this does not detract from Calvin's conviction that the Bible *is* in the full sense the word of God,[15] a Word, however, in which the Spirit has voluntarily dimmed His glory by the veil of humanity. Thus, Paul's 'failures in reasoning' do not diminish the heavenly wisdom, but 'it is rather by special Providence of God that under the despicable lowliness of the words, we are taught these lofty mysteries',[16] so that our faith may not be founded upon human eloquence. Evidently, in the Reformer's opinion there is a parallel between the lowliness of the Word made flesh and that of the Word that became Scripture.

When commenting on 1 Cor. 1:7[17] ('For Christ sent me . . . to preach the gospel: not with wisdom of words, lest the cross of Christ should be made of none effect'), he says that the human arts (rhetoric included) are excellent gifts of the Holy Ghost, and should not be condemned as contrary to piety; nevertheless, if Paul had preached the Cross with philosophical acuteness and rhetorical adornment, it would have lost its force and its sting; it has to be accepted without any diminution of its offence.[18]

Since Paul's epistles, though the Word of God, are at the same time also the words of St. Paul, Calvin feels free to criticize their style and language and even points out the time-bound character of some of Paul's injunctions. The warning against wearing the hair long[19] he reduces to the fact that the Greeks considered this effeminate, so that Paul took the old custom for 'nature', though in Paul's time in Germany and France it would have been considered shameful to cut the hair[20]. On one occasion even the possibility of a factual error in the original text is admitted: 'it evidently is an error . . . therefore this place ought to be corrected'.[21] And we are then also admonished to take heed of the important message instead of anxiously bothering about one word.[22] Thus, in sharp contrast to Bellarmine's conception, the possibility of an error 'ex parte dicentis' is not excluded.[23]

A great advantage of Calvin's exegesis was that in dubious cases he was not prone to make apodictical statements. For this reason John Donne preferred him to Melanchthon: 'Calvin will say, *Videtur*, It seems to be thus; Melanchthon, It can be no otherwise but thus. But the best men are but Problematical, onely the Holy Ghost . . . seales with Infallibility.' Praise such as this would be the highest praise one could bestow on a scientist as well. This sort of exegesis of the Book of Scripture set an example to those who occupied themselves with the interpretation of the Book of Nature.

It is to Calvin's credit that, though recognizing the discrepancy between the scientific world system of his day and the biblical text, he does not repudiate the results of scientific research on that account. Now if the Aristotelian or the Ptolemaic system, though not in the Bible, might nevertheless be true, then attempts to argue from the Bible for the rejection of other astronomical systems also become valueless. It then becomes possible to admit that the Copernican system, too, might be true without being in the Bible.

Here again prejudice has blinded historiographers: it would not fit in with the current image of Calvin if he opens the way to anything but intolerance and biblicism. According to A. D. White,[24] 'Calvin took the lead (against Copernicanism) in his Commentary on Genesis, by condemning all who asserted that the earth is not at the centre of the universe. He clinched the matter by the usual reference to the first verse of the ninety-third psalm, and asked, "Who will venture to place the authority of Copernicus above that of the Holy Spirit?" '[25]. White evidently borrowed this latter quotation from Farrar's '*History of Interpretation*'.[26]

'There is no lie so good as the precise and well-detailed one', and this one has been repeated again and again, quotation-marks included, by writers on the history of science, who evidently did not make the effort to verify the statement. For fifteen years, I have pointed out in several periodicals concerned with the history of science that the 'quotation' from Calvin is imaginary and that Calvin never mentioned Copernicus;[27] but the legend dies hard. It seems strange that Farrar, who in the body of his work did full justice to the scholarly character of Calvin's method of exegesis,[28] could go so far astray in the Introduction. I became suspicious of his statement because it does not fit in with Calvin's exegetical principles and because a parallel quotation allegedly from the Independent divine John Owen could immediately be proven to be spurious.[29]

Much stress is often laid on Luther's attitude in order to corroborate the statement that the Reformers and the Protestants, because of their biblicism, were in general less favourably inclined towards Copernicus' system than the Roman church before the condemnation of Galileo. Luther indeed in one of his table-talks rejected the opinion of an astronomer according to whom the sun was standing still, as a mistaken effort to be original: 'I believe Holy Scripture, for Joshua told the sun to stand still, not the earth'. But in his authorized works, Luther never mentioned the problem; it was just a commonsense remark, made when only rumours about Copernicus' work (not even his name is mentioned in the reminiscence of the reporter) were circulating (1539), and it was only printed (from the memory of one of his guests) twenty-seven years afterwards (1566).[30] So this attitude could hardly have exerted much influence, the more so as it does not play a role in Lutheran doctrine.

Only Melanchthon, who always remained faithful to Aristotelian philosophy, at first condemned the doctrine of the motion of the earth, and said that the magistrates ought to punish its proclamation.[31] But one year afterwards, in his second edition, this passage was omitted. Melanchthon was on very friendly terms with Petreius, the printer of Copernicus' work, and in an oration (1549) on his lately dead friend Caspar Cruciger (1504-1548), he mentioned that the latter was an admirer of Copernicus.[32] Moreover, he gave protection to Rheticus, Copernicus' only immediate pupil.[33a]

c. *Influence of Calvin's Accommodation Theory*

Undoubtedly, Calvin's accommodation theory had a considerable influence with Copernican astronomers in Protestant countries. In the preface to William Gilbert's *De Magnete* (1600) Edward Wright defended the theory concerning the motion of the earth (which had been put forward also by Gilbert himself), as not being in conflict with Scripture. Against literalist objections to the theory he repeated the argument that it was not the intention of Moses or the prophets to make known mathematical and physical subtleties, and therefore they did not enter into superfluous particulars. Moses 'accommodated himself to the understanding and the way of speech of the common people, like nurses to little children'.[33b] This was similar to Calvin's saying that the Holy Ghost 'chose rather after a sort to stammer with us, than to shut up the way of learning from the vulgar and unlearned sort'.[34]

The Reformed minister Philips van Lansbergen (1561–1632), a strict Calvinist, and a famous astronomer, was the most zealous propagator of Copernicanism in the Netherlands. He took the view (1619; 1629) that Scripture does not speak about astronomical matters 'according to the real situation but according to appearances'. The testimony of Scripture, so he said, is truth itself, but its authority was wrongly adduced to demonstrate the motion of the heavens; 'Scripture is given by inspiration of God, and is profitable for doctrine, for reproof, for correction, for instruction in righteousness, but it is not meet for instruction in geometry and astronomy'.[35] The method of calculating the circumference of the circle might be learnt from Archimedes, but not from Scripture, which often makes an approximate rather than an exact use of numbers, as for example where it is stated that the brazen sea was three cubits in diameter and a line of ten cubits compassed it round about.[36] In 1633, his son, the physician Jacob van Lansbergen, wrote a work in defence of his father who had been attacked by the Antwerp priest Fromondus and many others. In support of his father's view on the Bible, Jacob explicitly referred to 'our Calvin', *Calvinus noster*, and he approvingly quoted the relevant passages from the Reformer's writings: 'the Spirit, as it were, stammers with us', and also the commentary on Psalm 58, which said that the Holy Spirit accommodates Himself to the vulgar errors.[37]

Johannes Kepler, too, was, like his teacher in Tübingen, the theologian–astronomer Michael Mästlin, a convinced Copernican. But, being accused of crypto-calvinism, he could hardly be expected to quote Calvin. His exegetical arguments in support of the orthodoxy of the Copernican cosmology, however, did not differ much from those of the Reformer.[38]

d. *Galileo on Scripture and the Motion of the Earth*

Galileo's position on the relation between biblical exegesis and scientific theory was more complicated than that of the Protestants. Either his loyalties were divided or he just pretended to conform to the Counter-Reformation standpoint. Like Calvin, Kepler and Lansbergen, he accepted the accommodation theory, though only at a superficial level; for at the same time he adhered to the Roman-Catholic conception that the scientific 'truth' is in the bible, though (in his opinion) only visible to the initiated. He used the argument of accommodation when he discussed Church Fathers such as Augustine or Jerome, and Thomas Aquinas (who, however, never applied it to astronomical problems), who had pointed out that Scripture refers to God as having hands, being angry, etc. In Galileo's opinion it would be blasphemous to take this in the literal sense. Similarly, Scripture adapts itself to the common belief when speaking about the 'movement' of the sun.[39] In taking the Bible as authoritative only in matters of faith and morals[40], Galileo's standpoint coincided with that of Kepler and other protestant astronomers.

Yet Calvin's view that the Bible is 'a book for laymen' could hardly be fully shared by Galileo, who as a Roman Catholic was bound to recognize Tradition and the teaching authority of popes and councils. Therefore, though holding that Scripture accommodates itself to the opinion of the vulgar when speaking about natural things, he recognized on the other hand (probably not wholly sincerely) that the decisions of the pope on scientific issues in relation to the Bible should be humbly accepted.[41] But he pretended to expect that the Church authorities would never proclaim any verdict on matters of science and the Bible, without following the advice of the scientists. He must have known better, as it was extremely improbable at that time that laymen would be asked by the hierarchy how to interpret biblical texts.

At first sight it seems strange that Galileo thought he would find support for his Copernican standpoint in the Bible, as Scripture was said to use non-scientific language. He believed, however, that Scripture has also a deeper meaning, so that his ultimate standpoint did not *essentially* differ from that of his opponents. In his opinion, for the really initiated scholars, *astronomical truth* (that is the Copernican system) is in fact contained in the Bible. Apart from the seemingly plain meaning, there is a more profound one, hidden from the multitude. When Joshua said: 'Sun, stand thou still', the sun '*stood still* in the midst of heaven' instead of *revolving* on its axis in the midst of heaven. In Galileo's theory the consequence of the cessation of the sun's rotation would be that the earth would itself move more slowly and the day would become longer.[42] That is, at the time he wrote this, Galileo believed (or pretended to believe) that his discoveries (real or imaginary) concerning the rotation of the sun, and the theory that this rotation is the cause of the movement of the planets, were hidden within the biblical text and thus contributed to its better interpretation.

In the same way Galileo's interpretation of Psalm XIX, 5–7 (the sun like a bridegroom comes out of his chamber) was not that this is an accommodation to immediate observation, worded in poetic language, but that it means that the sun emits rays, a spirit spreading throughout the whole world and called 'bridegroom' because of its fertilizing power. 'He rejoices as a giant to run a race' refers to the emission of the rays, which takes place with as it were a bounding movement, and also to their great velocity and force and their capacity for penetrating all things. 'Coming out of his chamber' implies that not the solar body, but the light whereof the sun is the storeroom, is meant. 'The law of the Lord is perfect, converting the soul', means that God's spotless Law is as much more perfect than the sun, which is marked with stains (sunspots), as the power to guide souls is higher than the sun's power of moving the celestial bodies.[43] That is, Galileo assumed that the psalmist was making use of the heliocentric system together with the seventeenth century discoveries of sunspots and the rotation of the sun, as well as the theory of Kepler and Galileo which supposed that the sun's rotation provides the moving force of the planets. Here even a poetic passage received from Galileo a literalist interpretation, which, moreover, projected into the Bible not a generally received or an ancient world picture, but early seventeenth-century discoveries and hypotheses.

In Galileo's view then, Scripture, which at first sight was accommodating itself to the vulgar opinion on the world system, was using this opinion as a veil through which the learned could perceive scientific truth. At the same time he entrusted the final exegesis of such biblical texts to the hands of enlightened scientists. The supposed conformity of the two Books, Scripture and Nature, which led the literalists to the condemnation of the Copernican system, served Galileo for its verification, and in this respect he used the same method as his opponents.

e. *John Wilkins on Bible and Science*

A rather different approach was chosen by the ardent

Copernican and Puritan John Wilkins (1638; 1640), who repeatedly referred to Calvin's commentaries on Genesis and the Psalms,[44] and once also to 'our Country-man Master Wright', in support of his non-literalist interpretation of Scripture when touching on scientific matters. Of course, any appeal to the ancients too would be discarded by this staunch supporter of 'New Philosophy': 'it is not Aristotle but Truth, that should be the Rule of our Opinion'[45]. No less energetic was his opposition to those who 'look for any Secrets of Nature from the Words of Scripture, or will examine all its Expressions by the exact Rules of Philosophy'[46]

This verdict was aimed at the philosophers and theologians of the old school as well as at the adherents of a Mosaic or 'Hermetic' science: 'We must not be too bold with Divine Truths, or bring Scripture to patronize any Fancy of our own, though, (perhaps) it be a Truth'.[47] Wilkins, adhering to this point of view, found neither Aristotelianism nor his own Copernicanism in the Bible; on scientific matters the Holy Ghost did not express things as they 'are in themselves, but according to their appearances, and as they are conceived in common opinion'.[48]

Yet, when compared with the position taken by Calvin, there was a shift of emphasis. Calvin had spoken of an accommodation to the naive world picture, as when 'two great lights' are mentioned in Genesis, though the astronomers know that they are relatively small bodies. He had recognized the relative truth (the truth in daily life) of the biblical expressions for people of all times. Even Kepler had stressed that 'our senses, too, have their own kind of truth'.[49]

An unimaginative conception of truth was however gradually creeping into philosophy during the seventeenth century. People with the qualities of Kepler became more and more rare among both scientists and theologians. The meaning of 'truth' narrowed down to almost Euclidean deductions or to congruity with the scientific world picture. Even 'appearances to the senses' were considered to be 'vulgar *errors*', because they did not agree with what was considered by the scientists to be the objective reality.

For the scientist Galileo, metaphorical terms like 'God's hands' and the naive way of speech about the motion of the sun both belonged to the category of *erroneous* vulgar conceptions. The theologian Wilkins used the same word, 'error', for both. One of his propositions runs as follows: 'That the Holy Ghost, in many places in Scripture, does plainly conform his expressions unto the Errors of our Conceits, and does not speak of diverse Things as they are in themselves, but as they appear to us'.[50] Wilkins certainly did not conclude that Scripture, in doing this, was 'teaching' errors, but nevertheless, one has the impression that the profound sense of the beauty of nature and the almost mystical experience of a divine revelation in the creatures, which was still so strong with Kepler, is by this time fading away, to be replaced by what Boyle would call 'a rational worship'. It is revealing that Wilkins, like his friends Seth Ward and William Petty, felt little sympathy for metaphor.[51] In the 'philosophical language', propounded in his *Essay towards a real Character, and a philosophical Language* (1668), he did not provide for words for any creation of 'erring' imagination, such as fairies.

According to Wilkins, the expression in Psalm XIX, 5–6, 'The sun like a bridegroom cometh out of its chamber', refers perhaps to 'the conceit of ignorant people, as if it took rest all the while it was absent from us, and came out of its Chamber when it arose'. Here again, he stressed the 'erroneous' character of metaphors. How far the gratuitous conceptions of his own time set the standard of Wilkins' exegesis becomes evident when he says that the expression 'there is nothing hid from the Heat thereof', was used 'still in reference to the common Mistake, as if the Sun were actually hot in itself; and as if the Heat of the Weather were not generated by reflection, but did immediately proceed from the Body of the Sun'.[52] Whereas Galileo projected his private, modern conceptions *into* the biblical texts, Wilkins did the reverse and thought it necessary to state that his private scientific opinion was *not* to be found there. However, it must at least be reckoned to his credit that although he would not admit Scriptural arguments for the old system, equally he would not try to use them for his own purposes. When he explicitly opposed Galileo's maintenance of a hidden scientific meaning in Joshua's command: 'Sun, stand thou still',[53] Wilkins pointed out that the whole passage conforms to the appearance of things and to our grosser conceit. As for the phrase 'the sun stood still in the midst of heaven', this also must be interpreted with reference to the opinion of the ordinary people, and it is to be understood to mean a place near to neither east nor west.[54] It should be emphasized that these and other instances of accommodation do not in the least lessen Wilkins' acceptance of Scripture as divinely inspired and also his acceptance of the historical truth of the wonders, such as the 'supernatural eclipse' at Jesus' death.[55]

Wilkins was not so apodictic as most Copernicans about the 'truth' of the new system. He said that this system had proved that there are 'many strong Probabilities why the Sun should be in the midst of the world',[56] and he thought that no other system could so well be reconciled with appearances[57] but he affirmed only 'that ('tis probable) our Earth is one of the Planets'[58] (1640), as he had affirmed before (1638) 'that ('tis probable) there may be another habitable World in the Moon'.[59] If this last thought may disappoint the modern reader, who lets his appreciation of our ancestors depend on their 'foreknowledge' of *our* truths, he may find some compensation perhaps in noting that Wilkins added 'a discourse concerning the Possibility of a Passage thither'.

f. *Copernicans and Anti-Copernicans amongst the Reformed*[60]

1. *The Netherlands.* Calvin's scholarly approach to Bible interpretation had evidently exerted a liberating influence. But the members of the Reformed Churches were under no obligation whatever to follow his lead; 'calvinist' was to them a nickname invented to detract from their claim that their creed was 'catholic' because it was biblical. While asserting the right to choose the new philosophy they did not give up the right to cling to the old one. For a long time the majority, educated in scholastic philosophy (which during the sixteenth and seventeenth centuries continued to be predominant in the universities), held to the old system, either from conviction or from inertia because they were not interested in scientific problems.

Amongst the members of the Reformed Church the first rector of the University of Utrecht, Gisbertus Voet (1588–1676) took a conservative stand in matters of science and the Bible. He thought scholastic philosophy the only one conformable to Scripture. Moreover, in his opinion, 'Holy Scripture teaches not only what is necessary to salvation, but also lays down . . . the principles of all other good sciences and arts'.[61] That is, he rejected the opinion that the 'teaching' (the revelation in the proper sense) was limited to matters of faith and ethics as Lansbergen believed, and as Galileo did occasionally, and he was close to the position of the Roman theologians who claimed 'inerrancy' of scripture in scientific matters too.[62] According to Voet, Psalm XIX contains not poetical, but historical, factual truth; the Copernican system is therefore in flat contradiction to the text and the intention of the Bible. If the Holy Ghost were to accommodate Himself to the common people, He would tell a lie on behalf of the common people.[63]

Evidently, Voetius' unimaginative interpretation ran parallel to the pious blackmail of his great opponent René Descartes, who said that our mathematical principles must be right, because God could not *deceive* us. This statement reveals the same sort of rationalistic, 'euclidean' narrowing down of the concept of Truth, as if there were no poetic and no 'naive' truth which could be appreciated as well as 'scientific' truth. Small wonder, then, that when advising beginners in theology on commentaries on Genesis which they should read, this "Calvinist" kept silent about Calvin's commentary, but recommended that of B. Pereira, S.J., one of the Conimbricenses.[64] Calvin's accommodation theory was precisely the sort of reasoning that Voet opposed as much as possible.

Such opposition as that of Voet in Holland or of Alexander Ross in England, however, had no great effect. In general, theologians who had a real interest in astronomy were not affected by it. In the Netherlands the most influential Reformed theologian of the beginning of the seventeenth century, André Rivet, was favourably inclined towards Copernicanism. The well-known scientist Dr. Isaac Beeckman co-operated with Lansbergen; their common pupil, Martinus Hortensius, who became a professor in Amsterdam, was, as mentioned earlier, an outspoken Copernican. The secretary of the Dordrecht synod, Daniel Heinsius, and the pensionary Jacob Cats wrote laudatory poems on Lansbergen's defence of Copernicanism. In strictly orthodox

Zeeland, the States granted a pension to Lansbergen so that he could devote all his time to his astronomical studies. The Catholic theologian, Libertus Fromondus of Antwerp, spoke deprecatingly of the 'calvinistic-copernican' system of his opponent Lansbergen and pointed out that among seafarers only the Hollanders and Zeelanders and not the Portuguese adhered to the Copernican system. He omitted, however, to mention *why* there were no Copernicans among the latter, though the reason could be found on the title page of his own book announcing the refutation of Lansbergen's astronomy and the vindication of the decrees of the Holy Office.

2. *England.* The English Puritans have the reputation of professing a most rigorous biblicism, so that one might have expected the idea of the motion of the earth to have been unanimously repudiated by them. Their biblicism, however, was primarily concerned with the mode of worship, with church government and with morals. Nevertheless, it may be assumed that those among them who had no particular scientific interest took up the same position as the influential Independent theologian, John Owen, who opposed Copernicanism on biblical grounds. On the other hand, it is remarkable how many staunch defenders of the theory of the motion of the earth were to be found among those English Puritans who were actively interested in the science of their day. Edward Wright (1600) and Nathanael Carpenter (1627) accepted only the daily rotation, which was precisely the point at issue in the debate about biblical interpretation. Consequently, their arguments did not differ from those of the adherents of a fully Copernican system. Carpenter defended the 'philosophical liberty' of accepting a theory of the motion of the earth, over against 'those precise men' who 'will condemne without examination, and sticke to the

plaine letter, notwithstanding all absurdities'.[65] Robert Recorde (who wrote before the term 'puritanism' arose) had already hinted in 1556 that Copernicus might be right. The Puritan Thomas Digges not only defended the Copernican system (1573), but in 1576 he went even further, when he propounded the idea of an infinite universe, with the fixed stars at varying distances beyond the orb of Saturn. Digges thus broke through the notion of a closed universe which even Kepler was to uphold. Amongst the Puritans who were wholly committed to the Copernican system were Mark Ridley (1560–1624), Dr. John Bainbridge (1618), the Gresham Professors Henry Briggs (1561–1630, of Logarithm fame) and Henry Gellibrand (1597–1636), the famous mathematician John Wallis, and, perhaps most zealous of all, John Wilkins.

The relatively strong position of Copernicanism and New Philosophy in general in the Protestant countries is emphasized by the tendency of Roman Catholics themselves more or less to identify Copernicanism and Protestantism, as when Froidmont spoke of the 'calvinistic-copernican' system. In 1624 one of the cardinals cautioned the pope to be careful about a decision on Copernicus' system, as all heretics adhered to his opinion and held it for certain.[66] Galileo, too, believed that 'all the most distinguished heretics' accepted this doctrine.[67] It may be that his correspondence with Kepler and with his friend Elia Diodati had given him this impression, but of course he knew that the Catholic priests Gassendi and Mersenne in France and quite a few sympathizers in Italy were also on his side, though after his trial he no doubt felt it wise not to mention their names in a letter.

There was, of course, at that time no cogent proof for the reality of the movement of the earth. Therefore, a scholar's refusal fully to accept it is not always a mark of conservatism or even backwardness. Galileo himself was of the opinion that his (dubious) explanation of the tides in particular gave a factual demonstration of the truth of the daily rotation, but Isaac Beeckman would have preferred to have a mechanical model for testing the theory before unreservedly asserting its truth. The point at issue is whether the theory was rejected after an appeal to philosophical or even to theological arguments and prejudices, or exclusively after comparing the different systems and judging them on their own intrinsic scientific merits. Assuming the latter position, the wisest course at that time would have been to proclaim the hypothesis of the motion of the earth not as a scientific dogma but only as a most probable theory (as was done by Beeckman and Pascal).

At any rate, even in the sixteenth and seventeenth centuries, the decision was one that had better not be made by an ecclesiastical authority. This, in spite of his assertions of obedient acceptance of the decision of the Roman See, was in fact Galileo's opinion too. Having declared that the Pope had an absolute power to admit or to condemn a thesis, even if it did not concern a matter of faith, he annihilated his own admission by adding that no creature has the power to make theses false or true when they are not so according to their nature and in fact.[68] Pascal, more openly, flatly denied the right of church authorities to decide on scientific issues when he told the Jesuits: 'It was also in vain that you did obtain that decree of Rome against Galileo which condemned his opinion touching the motion of the earth, for that will not prove that the earth is standing still, and if one had solid observations demonstrating that she does turn round, the whole of mankind together would neither be able to prevent the earth from turning round nor themselves from turning round also, with her.'[69] Pascal's work, however, was put on the Index, and Roman Catholic theologians in general had to take up a position opposed to Copernicus, either from personal conviction, or—as Wilkins put it— from fear of deviating from the exegesis as given by 'the supposed infallible Church'.

C. PURITANISM AND SCIENCE

a. *The Character of Puritanism*

In the sixteenth and seventeenth centuries in England the relationship between Puritanism and science was close. Now and again this fact has been denied, particularly by those English authors in whom the anti-Puritan feelings of the Restoration period still linger. By narrowing down the definition of 'Puritanism' so that it includes none but a rather small group of Independents of the 1640s, it is argued that the majority of scientists of that epoch were not Puritans. Puritanism, however, by no means always excluded loyalty to the established church, nor did it include all Calvinists. During the first part of Elizabeth's reign especially, the theology of the Church of England was strongly Calvinistic. Many of the archbishops and bishops before Laud, who was Archbishop of Canterbury in Charles I's reign, were 'Calvinists' in theology; even Archbishop Whitgift, a man usually hostile to Puritans, showed himself to be decidedly Calvinist in his Lambeth declaration (1595) on predestination. The Church, however, maintained a sober ritual and an episcopal government and for Calvin himself neither episcopacy nor ceremonies were obstacles to unity.

The Puritans (the name first appeared in the 1560s) were more radical; they wanted either no bishops at all, or else bishops who were not prelates but only superintendents.

They insisted on regular preaching instead of an elaborate liturgy; they wished to remodel the church on what they believed to be the express teaching of the New Testament, whereas the other party admitted also practices and standards of behaviour that were not expressly *forbidden* by Holy Scripture. In almost every other respect Elizabethan Puritans did not essentially differ from other English Protestants of the same period; it was mainly a matter of degree. The topics on which they disagreed were of such a kind that affiliation to the Puritan cause did not always show itself in an unequivocal way in scientific works. Since many outstanding people of those days were sympathetic to some of the Puritan tenets rather than fully committed to all their ideas, it is easier now to say whether a particular person was decidedly anti-Puritan rather than to establish which men were Puritan. The problem is made more difficult by the fact that the latter would not call themselves by that name.[1]

Before the 1640s, then, the most progressive part of the Church of England might be considered 'puritan'. After that time the word Puritan covered everyone from 'non-prelatical' Episcopalians and Presbyterians to the Independents and that latter party's left wing (Baptists, Quakers, Fifth Monarchy men), members of which might be considered as separatists. Moreover, whereas in the Elizabethan period there were many non-puritan Calvinists, during the Commonwealth some of the left-wing sects were non-Calvinistic in their theology.[2] But all of them had in common their low-church tendencies and their emphasis on the priesthood of all believers. Of course, the same tensions could be found among them as existed among continental Protestants of the time and even within the medieval church: there were rationalistic and pietistic currents, and also different attitudes as to the relations between civil and church authority.

In discussions on the origins of the Royal Society, a distinction has sometimes been made between the adherents of the 'new philosophy' and the 'enthusiasts'. The latter, in their dislike of the classical 'heathenish' heritage, not only rejected Aristotelian natural philosophy, but also sought an alternative in a natural science (physics, chemistry) founded on biblical texts. As pointed out above, they in fact resorted to hermetic, theosophical and Paracelsist traditions.[3] The more moderate Protestants, on the basis of the doctrine of 'common grace', accepted a large part of the ancient heritage, but (except for the strongly conservative) they wanted to go further than the ancients, especially in science. Rejecting an allegedly 'Mosaic' science, they shared with the radicals the conviction that science in the last resort should be founded on the most ancient authority, that is on the book of nature itself.

Between the two groups, however, there was no hard and fast dividing line. Richard Bostocke (1585), who was a member of one of Elizabeth's Parliaments, compared the religious reformers such as Wycliffe, Luther, Zwingli and Calvin with the scientific reformers, pointing out that both returned to truly 'auncient' learning, the former to the Book of Scripture and the latter to the Book of Nature. Among the latter Bostocke reckoned Copernicus (who, however as a 'Pythagorean' could hardly be considered more 'biblical' in his astronomy than could Ptolemy), as well as Paracelsus, who was thought to have restored 'Mosaic' science and who, in any case, was hostile to the Greek philosophers. On the other hand Thomas Tymme (1612), known as a translator of Calvin, was on biblical grounds favourably inclined to Paracelsus, but was *against* Copernicus.

In the seventeenth century, John Webster (a left wing Independent with Leveller inclinations) indiscriminately praised Copernicus, Paracelsus, Descartes, and also Epicurean philosophy as brought to light by Gassendi. Samuel Hartlieb and John Amos Comenius showed characteristics of religious 'enthusiasm' as well as rationalistic and Baconian traits. These trends should not be contrasted too sharply. Hartlieb's connections were with the radicals as well as with the moderates. The Cambridge Platonists, of whom Ralph Cudworth was one, combined spiritualistic and rationalistic tendencies.[4] Ramus and Bacon were not favourably inclined towards Paracelsus and 'Mosaic' science, but nevertheless they believed, like the Paracelsists, in the wisdom of the 'Egyptians' and of the Pythagoreans. Even some of the protagonists of the new, corpuscular or atomic philosophy, such as Boyle or Newton, believed in the wisdom of the 'most ancient' philosophers and alchemists.

The 'new philosophy' was, on the one hand, an anti-Aristotelian (that is corpuscular, atomic, chemical) doctrine, and on the other hand, a science based on 'manual experiments' which recognized Francis Bacon as its prophet. Many 'corpuscularians', among them Basso, Sennert, Jungius and Boyle, saw that chemistry had opened the way for them by propagating the use of the hands in scientific investigation and by inevitably leading to corpuscular theories. The pietistic stress on religious experience ran parallel to that on experience as the basis of science. It is true that with some chemical philosophers, though by no means with all, 'scientific experience' bore a somewhat mystical character. Thus the radicals Biggs, Webster and Hall, who advocated the introduction of chemistry into the universities, may have wanted to introduce 'hermetic' and Paracelsan teachings as well, but what they expressly emphasized was the *experi-*

mental character of that discipline, and in this they were the allies of the more soberminded advocates of the new science such as Wilkins.

Undoubtedly, as in every vanguard movement, there were fanatics among the Puritans; but on the other hand they, like all their contemporaries, carried on some medieval traditions. The late Professor C. S. Lewis, writing on sixteenth-century Puritanism, pointed out that it is 'an absurd idea' that the Puritans were 'somehow grotesque, elderly people, outside the main current of life'. 'In their own day they were, of course, the very latest thing. Unless we can imagine the freshness, the audacity, and (soon) the fashionableness of Calvinism, we shall get our whole picture wrong.[5]

b. *Puritan Baconianism*

Puritanism found many adherents among the newly emancipated class of merchants, artisans and navigators, a class that was on the move and showed much interest in science and technology. Gresham College, their meeting place with scholars, was known as a hotbed of Puritanism, and it is understandable that the writings of that great advocate of science and technology, Francis Bacon, were popular in these circles. Francis Bacon, though no Puritan himself, had been educated in the spirit of Elizabethan Puritanism, as his religious creed showed, and this spirit was, as Spedding remarked, *incorporated* in his theory of the world. The whole scheme of Christian theology—creation, fall, mediation and redemption—underlay his philosophical works; there was hardly any kind of argument into which it did not at one time or another introduce itself.[6] This philosophy fitted in perfectly with the ideals of the Puritans, especially of those radicals among them who wanted to christianize, though not to clericalize, every department of life. Moreover, their un-Baconian disobedience to authorities in the church, and afterwards in the state, ran parallel to a similar attitude towards authority in science,[7] an attitude that in the latter case was certainly Baconian. Finally, Bacon's quasi-biblical language must have appealed to his English contemporaries in general and to his Puritan fellow-citizens in particular. Many of his characteristic terms and slogans are met with again and again in their writings: 'advancement of learning', 'discovery of a new world', 'further reformation', 'light'.

In 1649 John Hall sent a 'humble motion' to Parliament, 'concerning the advancement of learning and the reformation of the universities'. Now that the reformation of the state and the church had been accomplished, he asked for 'this last piece of reformation'[8].

For English Puritans of the seventeenth century the Kingdom of Man supplemented the Kingdom of God; after reason had submitted itself to divine Truth, learned piety and pious learning would lead to a 'sublime knowledge'. It was a time of great expectations. The discovery of a new geographical world in the past century would lead, according to Francis Bacon, to the discovery of a new intellectual world. John Wilkins in his discourse proving 'that there may be another habitable world in the Moon' and 'the possibility of a voyage thither' (1638) even anticipated the discovery of a new world in the heavens. Bacon had condemned Aristotle's opinion that Man could only *imitate* nature, or *help* her to finish her work, but could never *emulate* her. Wilkins now distinguished between the arts that imitate nature, those that help her, and those that conquer and surpass her. To him, the arts belonging to the third category were the most excellent, as they had the highest aim—to take away the curse from labour and to restore man's dominion over nature.[9]

The innovators in the field of science were also interested in a universal and efficient language which would make scientific and scholarly communication more easy, helping in the propagation of religion and facilitating commerce. After the fall, so they said, two general curses had been inflicted on mankind: labour became a toilsome burden, and languages a confusion. The restoring of the Kingdom of Man, made possible in principle by Christ, would mean then a 'new' science, implying both dominion over nature and a scientific, clear and easy language, to remedy the confusion of Babel.[10]

c. An 'Age of Light'

Utopian and eschatological expectations rose high during the Puritan Revolution. Christ's Kingdom would be established on the earth as a preparation for its final dissolution. After the Civil War there was a widespread belief that the Age of Light had begun in science and religion, in worldly and spiritual matters. England would be the model to the rest of the world. 'I see ... a noble and puissant Nation rousing herself like a strong man after sleep ... I see her as an Eagle ... purging ... her long abused sight at the fountain itself of heavenly radiance.' 'For now the time seems come, wherein Moses the great Prophet may sit in heaven, rejoicing to see that memorable and glorious work of his fulfilled, when not only our seventy Elders but all the Lord's people are becoming Prophets'.[11] Milton's call was a parallel to the injunction laid by Bacon and by Boyle on all travellers, mariners and tradesmen, to join the enterprise of building up a Natural History of the world as a basis for a 'free philosophy'. Men hoped that social justice would become established, disease and disaster would disappear, thanks to the new science of which Bacon had prophesied and which had its beginning, evidently, from 'God, the Father of Light'.[12]

Comenius wrote his *Way of Light* (1642) in England. In the evening of the world knowledge would become general, as prophesied by Zachariah in the words: 'It shall come to pass, that at evening it shall be light'.[13] On the last day of the week of creation God brought forth 'the intellectual light, the spirit of man, which is called the lamp of the Lord'.[14] Similarly, at the end of the world the 'highest stage of light' will appear. The Day of the Universal Light, when the Monarchy of Christ would be established, was drawing near and *we* have to offer our humble aid to God, if He will perhaps deign to use it and cause that supreme light to rise upon us all the more quickly. 'Surely, then, when we hope and pray to God for the restoration of a ruined world at the coming of that longed-for age of light, we must understand that at the same time we ourselves are pledged to hasten its coming'. 'No man should refuse his aid to God, if he believes that he has any gift or inspiration by which he may be of service to man.' In Comenius' scheme this implies the further-ance of science and technology in order to alleviate the burden of life, as well as the improvement of teaching and the spread of the Gospel in order to make men 'more enlightened'[15a].

Seven years later John Hall (1627–1656) believed that this fullness of time was imminent; the age of light, he said, has come, an age full of miracle, which chases the shadows before the coming of the Great Day, for 'it hath pleased the Sun of Righteousness[15b] to breake through the clouds...and to let us have more of day. And as the Sun here below doth not onely ... discover himselfe, but also guilds and discloses all about him, so that eternal Sun, when He opens himselfe, opens at the same time all humane and inferiour knowledge.

... Now, He having every day made greater appearance of himselfe, human learning hath also been more enlightened.'[16]

At first sight it may seem strange that people who fought so hard for the liberation of science from the tyranny of philosophers and clerics, held at the same time the conviction that religious and scientific enlightenment must go together, and that religion should penetrate, illuminate and revolutionize science. It should be realized, however, that to these people religion did not mean school theology, nor even official verdicts of church authorities. Their conviction was shared, though expressed in more soberminded terms, by such moderate people as Robert Boyle (a 'puritan at heart', if ever there was one, but at the same time a moderate royalist and episcopalian). Boyle and his friends, who wanted science to be free from the tutelage of metaphysical systems and who deemed the Bible no source for science, yet considered themselves, because of their new obedience to God's revelation, to be '*Christian* virtuosi'.

Puritanism and New Philosophy had thus much in common: anti-authoritarianism, optimism about human possibilities, rational empiricism, the emphasis on experience. Therefore 'the happy marriage of these two movements was based on an intrinsic compatibility' (Merton).[17] This does not necessarily imply that Puritanism as such produced many highly qualified scientists. The issue at stake here belongs to the sociology of religion: Did Puritanism in fact create a spiritual climate favourable to the cultivation and freedom of science? The affirmative answer to this question is no invention of modern sociologists.[18] The vindicators of the new science gave the same answer. John Wallis writing in 1669 to Boyle, describes how Dr. South had delivered a speech in Oxford of which the first part consisted of 'invectives against Cromwell, fanatics, the Royal

Society and New Philosophy . . . the last, of execrations against fanaticism, conventicles, comprehension and new philosophy.'[19] This meant that 'fanaticism' (Puritanism) and new learning were regarded by the conservatives as cognate vices. It was for this reason that the apologist of the Royal Society, Thomas Sprat, had to make such an effort to prove that there was no connection whatever between the two.

d. *'Enthusiasm' and Learning*

The solution found by Sprat and used by his followers until the present day was to sever the connection between the moderate Puritans—those who had now 'conformed' like John Wilkins (who became a bishop after the Restoration) and like Sprat himself—and the radicals, who had opposed the moderates as well as the conservatives and now had to bear the blame for all that had gone wrong during the Commonwealth period. These radicals had some affinity with the Anabaptists of the continent and were identified by their various opponents with the worst of the latter. The radicals deviated either in a rationalistic or in a spiritualistic direction, and they were accused of being 'against all learning'. This was, however, a serious and sometimes malevolent exaggeration. The main reason for this accusation was the violent controversy about the universities. The academies of the Reformation concentrated their efforts on training for a learned ministry. The need for this had been strongly argued by the Reformers against the Roman Church on the continent and by the early Puritans against the traditionalists in England. The Anabaptists of the continent and the left wing Puritans, on the other hand, feared the rise of a new danger, that of preferring a humanistic and theological training to a prophetic calling that could only be guaranteed by inspiration through the Holy Ghost. The tragic debate between the Polish Reformer Jan Laski (John a Lasco), an accomplished humanist who had been a friend of Erasmus, and Menno Simonsz, the simple village priest who had become an Anabaptist leader, clearly revealed the misunderstanding on both sides.[2]

In this controversy not only the traditionalists and the Presbyterians but also the Independents, like Joseph Sedgwick and Sydrach Simpson (one of the five 'dissenting brethren' of the Westminster Assembly), were on the side of a learned ministry. Sedgwick condemned that 'spirit of Enthusiasm and pretended Inspiration, that disturbs and strikes at the Universities' (1653).[21] He pointed out that 'the Reformation of Religion and the reviving of the Gentile learning' were contemporary and promoted by 'the same instruments'. It would be 'strange, if the Reformation, begun in Knowledge', could not otherwise be carried on than by returning to 'the ignorance of darker and more degenerate ages'. He even stated that genuine philosophy is 'God's discovery of himself to our understandings by the light of Reason and works of Creation',[22]—a first announcement of the rationalistic trend that would in the future lure many nonconformists away from orthodoxy. Simpson, at the same time, argued that 'when learning goes down, religion goes down too'.[23]

On the other hand, the so-called 'enthusiasts', with the exception of some ultra-spiritualists, Anabaptist millennarians and Fifth Monarchy Men, had nothing in principle against the advancement of learning or against thoroughly modernized university training, though they had quite a lot against the universities as they were at that time. The 'enthusiasts' had nothing against ministers who knew Hebrew and Greek, but they were against making this an indispensable condition by which even the Holy

Ghost would be bound when calling people to the ministry.

John Saltmarsh, one of the extreme protagonists of 'inner religion', was prepared to allow learning its place 'anywhere in the kingdom of the world, but not in the kingdom of God'.[24] Even the erudite John Milton, who had the greatest love for the classical tradition, agreed with this standpoint. He was against an established church and university training of the clergy and he reminded his readers that in the most ancient reformed church (the Waldensian) the ministers were apprenticed to a trade, in order not to be a burden to the church, and studied Scripture, 'which is the only true theology'.[25] Unlike the humanists Erasmus and Vives, he had no wish to substitute classical scholarship for scholastic philosophy in theological education.

The violent attacks on the universities by men like John Webster and William Dell, the Master of Caius College, were not inspired by any hatred of humane learning. Dell only opposed the latter when it was mixed with divinity. In his arguments Dell, 'who held the doctrine of the Inner Light with all the intensity of the Quakers', repeated much of what Luther had adduced against scholastic theology: 'Humane learning, mingled with divinity, or the Gospel of Christ understood according to Aristotle, hath begun, continued, and perfected the mystery of iniquity in the outward Church'.[26] This was a stock argument of all those who wanted a radically evangelical religion. Many of the controversies between Puritans and non-Puritans, or within the Puritan sects, made manifest the age-old and undying tension between Athens and Jerusalem, the two poles of the western spiritual heritage. The Fathers had wrestled with this problem; at the end of the eleventh century it came to the fore in the debate between Manegold of Lautenbach and

Wolfhelm of Cologne,[27] and the Christian humanists had sought to establish a new equilibrium.

The Puritan defenders of a 'prophetic' ministry held that neither the study of Aristotelian philosophy, nor a knowledge of Greek and Hebrew, was indispensable for preachers. Already in 1582 the father of English separatism, Robert Browne, had written 'against the abuse of tongues in preaching'. This attack was directed not against a scholarly translation of the Bible, but against the pedantic use of Latin and Greek quotations in sermons. Similarly he thundered against 'vayne logicke' in the exposition of Scripture. According to Browne, Solomon obtained his wisdom by studying and searching out things one by one, 'yes, by experience especially', but not by 'Rhetoricke and Logicke'. He was particularly irked by the fact that one had to study the heathenish philosophy of Aristotle before tackling the text of Scripture. Though there is no reason to suppose that he was at all interested in natural science, he spoke at least in a more positive vein about the astronomy of the Chaldeans than about the speculative philosophy of the Greeks.[28]

In general then the natural sciences, so seriously neglected in the universities, were positively appreciated by the critics of those institutions. Even those political extremists, Gerrard Winstanley the Digger, and William Walwyn the Leveller, wanted a reform of education that would give their due place to science and its applications. Winstanley's[29] educational curriculum consisted almost wholly of science and technology. He insisted on *experimental* knowledge in spiritual as well as natural matters, the latter making us 'to see and to know God (the Spirit of the whole Creation) in all His works' (1649). Walwyn (1646) had nothing against 'any kind of learning, except that part of it, which puffeth up'. He reminded his readers that Moses was skilful in all the learning of the Egyptians, 'which the Scriptures testifie without reproof, and S. Paul certainly read the poets'.[30] Again the Quakers in England, after the second half of the seventeenth century, took an active interest in applied science; and the Mennonites in the Netherlands, from the beginning of the seventeenth century, showed no trace of hostility to learning, as even their critic Voetius had to acknowledge.[31]

In spite of all this, 'Puritans' and 'Anabaptists' were accused of destroying all learning; their enemies maliciously identified each of these parties with their extreme left wing, and even the extremists and 'enthusiasts', with few exceptions, were misrepresented, since their 'hostility' was directed only towards scholastic theology and philosophy and did not include languages and sciences. How little ground there was for this accusation became evident when, after the Restoration, the Puritans were accused of precisely the reverse, of combining 'enthusiasm' with a reprehensible *love* for learning—learning, that is, of the wrong sort, *new* learning. At the same time, since Puritanism was in disgrace but the New Philosophy was now under royal patronage, the *defenders* of the new science now deemed it expedient to deny any connection with Puritanism by identifying the latter with those 'enthusiasts' who disliked learning. Thus one party blamed the Puritans for loving science too much, the opposite party accused them of destroying all learning.

These recriminations cannot, however, wipe out the fact that, in spite of their political annihilation, much of the influence of the Puritans remained. The Puritans, through the whole spectrum of their views from the right to the left, 'were the main support of the new science before the Restoration', and they left 'their indelible stamp on the next generation'.[32] No differences about the interpretation of the facts can impair the reality of the facts themselves, which have been brought to light by historico-sociological research and which prove that 'Puritanism, and ascetic protestantism generally . . . played no small part in arousing a sustained interest in science'.[33]

NOTES TO CHAPTER V

SECTION A

1. A. de Candolle, *Histoire des sciences et des savants*, 2ᵉ éd., Genève-Bâle, 1885, pp. 329–331.
2. J. Pelseneer, *La Réforme et le progrès des sciences en Belgique au XVI siècle* in: Science, Medicine, and History, Oxford, 1953, p. 281. *Les persécutions contre les savants en Belgique*, in: Le Flambeau, 1954 pp. 636 ff., and other publications.
3. D. Stimson, *Puritanism and the New Philosophy in Seventeenth-century England*, in: Bull. Inst. Hist. Medic. III (1935), pp. 321–334. R. K. Merton, *Science, Technology and Society in Seventeenth Century England*, in: Osiris, iv (1938), pp. 471–474.
4. M. Matthijssen, *Katholiek middelbaar onderwijs en intellectuele emancipatie. Een sociografische facetstudie van het emancipatie—vraagstuk der Katholieken in Nederland*. Thesis Nijmegen 1958, pp. 67, 200. This author is of the opinion that the results of de Candolle, combined with the many data collected in his own work on Western-European countries and the U.S.A., 'form a solid basis for the hypothesis, that this problem is general' (not restricted to the Netherlands). He claims to have demonstrated that the sociological theories (of Weber, Merton and others) 'are indeed founded on a reality' (*op. cit.*, p. 68).
5. J. J. Kane, in: American Catholic Sociolog. Review, 16 (1955), pp. 27–29. 'Catholics who attain eminence . . . are found mainly in three fields: religion, law and education'.
6. Agnes Arber, *Herbals*, 2d ed., Cambridge, 1953, p. 266.
6b. H. Fischer, *Conrad Gessner, Leben und Werk,* Zürich, 1965.
7. C. E. Raven, *English Naturalists from Neckam to Ray*, Cambridge, 1947, p. 127; cf. pp. 54, 91, 96.
8. The famous fifteenth-century astronomer Regiomontanus settled down in Nürnberg because it was an important meeting point of continental trade routes and possessed craftsmen with great skill in instrument-making.

9. Chr. Wren, *Parentalia*, ed. London, 1750, p. 206.

10. Cf. R. Hooykaas, *Humanisme, science et réforme—Pierre de la Ramée*, Leyden, 1958, pp. 95–96; 86–87.

11. M. Weber, *Gesammelte Aufsätze zur Religionssoziologie*, vol. I, Tübingen, 1920, pp. 83, 120, 124, 163.

12. Merton, *op. cit.*, p. 418.

13. Merton, *op. cit.*, p. 417: 'the sentiments with which the various Puritan sects were imbued, despite different rationalizations and theological views, led to approximately identical implications for social conduct'. Weber and Merton have stressed that for these sects 'similar ethical maxims may be correlated with very different dogmatic foundations'. Merton, *op. cit.*, p. 422.

14. Merton, *op. cit.*, p. 419. Cf. J. T. McNeill, *The History and Character of Calvinism*, New York, 1954, 1967, p. 222.

15. C. E. Raven, *Science and Religion*, Cambridge, 1953, p. 123. Cf. our review of this book (broadcast B.B.C., 3rd progr., 1954) in: Free Univ. Qu., 3 (1954), pp. 205–211.

   R. K. Merton, *op. cit.*, p. 417; cf. *op. cit.*, pp. 459, 432, n. 56. On Jansenism, Merton, *op. cit.*, p. 479 and S. F. Mason, *Main Currents of Scientific Thought*, New York, 1953, pp. 137, 140.

16. 'It is therefore the concernment of great persons (of the magistracy, the nobility, the gentry, of all persons that have any considerable interest in the world) who would safely and sweetly enjoy their dignity, power, or wealth, by all means to protect and promote piety as the best instrument of their security, and undisturbedly enjoying the accommodations of their state. 'Tis in all respects their best wisdom and policy; that will as well preserve their outward state here, as satisfy their consciences within, and save their souls hereafter' (Is. Barrow, *Works*, vol. I, Edinburgh, 1842, p. 11, *The Profitableness of Godliness*, 1 Timothy 4:8); '. . . success, . . ., wealth, honour, wisdom, virtue, salvation . . . are usually conveyed to us through our industry, as the ordinary channel and instrument of attaining them' (*op. cit.*, p. 479, *Of Industry in our general calling as Christians*, on Romans 12:11, 'not slothful in business'). McNeill, referring to this and other authors, rightly pointed out the unbalanced character of the argument of R. H. Tawney that traces the rise of economic individualism through Puritan writings alone (*op. cit.*, pp. 418–421).

17. *Heidelberg Catechism*, Sunday 25, qu. 65.

18. *Confessio Belgica*, art. 23 and 24. The Heidelberg Catechism, the Netherlands' Confession of Faith, and the Canones of Dordrecht are the official declarations of faith of the Reformed Churches in the Netherlands.

19. Volcker Coiter, *Externarum et internarum principalium humani corporis tabulae*, Noribergae, 1572, c. 3.

20. Cf. Arber, op. cit., p. 88.
21. B. Palissy, *Oeuvres*, éd. Anatole France, Paris, 1880: *Récepte véritable* (1564), pp. 35, 114.
22. Kepler to Herwart von Hohenberg, 26-III-1958.
23. *Confessio Belgica*, art. 2. See above, Ch. III, note 15, and: Francis Bacon, *The Advancement f Learning*, Bk. I.
24. J. Calvin, *Commentary on I Corinthians* (8:1).
25. J. Calvin, *Institutes*, I. 5.2: Nevertheless, according to the late Dr. C. E. Raven (*op. cit.*, p. 123), Calvin, by the strictness of his religious discipline, discouraged activities which did not make directly for the edification of the saints. R. K. Merton says that Calvin 'deprecated science'.
26. Calvin, *Commentary on Genesis* (1:16).
27. J. Kepler, *Astronomia Nova* (1609), Introductio.
28. On Calvin's belief in immutable law: Merton, *op. cit.*, p. 468 (following Hermann Weber, *Die Theologie Calvins*, Berlin, 1930, pp. 29, 31) and: S. F. Mason, *op. cit.*, pp. 142, 137.
29. See above, Ch. I, p. 12-13; Ch. II, pp. 32-35.
30. See above, Ch. I, on Malebranche and Berkeley. Also: W. J.'s Gravesande, *Oratio de Evidentia*, Leiden, 1724, pp. liv-lv.
31. C. S. Lewis, *English Literature in the Sixteenth Century*, Oxford, 1954, p. 49.
32. R. Hooykaas, *The Principle of Uniformity in Geology, Biology, and Theology*, Leiden, 1959[1], 1963[2], pp. 211, 225.
    R. Hooykaas, *Science and Theology in the Middle Ages*, in: Free Univ. Qu. (1954), paragr, 6, 7, 8, 12, 13.
33. See Ch. II, pp. 33-35 and pp. 36-38.
34. J. Calvin, *Institutes*, I, ch. 16, par. 4.
35. R. Hooykaas, *Science and Religion in the Seventeenth Century* (*Isaac Beeckman*) in: Free Univ. Qu., I (1951), p. 180.
    Isaac Beeckman, *Journal*, ed. C. de Waard, vol. I, p. 261 (1618); vol. II, p. 375 (1626).
36. A. Müller-Armack, *Genealogie der Wirtschaftsstile*, 3rd ed. Stuttgart, 1944, p. 119. For the nineteenth and twentieth centuries this has been advanced as a possible explanation of the lag in production of scientists by the Roman Catholic part of the population of U.S.A.: 'It may also be that leadership, even outside the purely religious field, is still considered a clerical prerogative and the same seems equally true of scholarship' (J. J. Kane, *The social structure of American Catholics*, in: The American Catholic Sociol. Rev., 16 (1955), p. 30).
37. B. Palissy, *Discours admirables de la nature des eaux et fontaines* (1580), 'Des Pierres'.
38. Beeckman, *Journal*, vol. IV, pp. 86ff. The role of ruling elders ('lay

elders') in the Reformed Churches and the injunction on the ministers (the 'teaching elders') that none of them shall rule over the others, and the principle of election (over against appointment from above) of the ministers, worked together in a non-clericalistic direction. On the other hand, R. H. Knapp and H. B. Goodrich, in their study on the *Origins of American Scientists* (Chicago, 1952), offer, in partial explanation of 'the conspicuously inferior position of virtually all Catholic institutions (in U.S.A.) in the production of scientists', amongst other reasons, that 'Catholicism has permitted comparatively little secularization of outlook among its constituents and has maintained a firm authoritarian structure' (*op. cit.*, p. 288).

39. W. Borough, *A Discourse of the Variation of the Compasse* (1581). Preface.
40. N. S. (=John Wilkins), *Vindiciae Academiarum*, London, 1654, pp. 1–2.
41. N. Carpenter, *Geographie Delineated Forth*, 2nd ed., Oxford, 1635, Bk. I, ch. 10.
42. P. Ramus, *Actiones duae habitae in senatu, pro regia mathematica professionis cathedra*, II (1566). Cf. R. Hooykaas, *Humanisme, science et réforme*, ch. iv ('La philosophie libre de Ramus'), pp. 15–19.
43. J. Kepler, *Astronomia Nova* (1609), Introductio.
44. J. Wilkins, *A Discourse concerning a new Planet* (1640), prop. I, consideration 1.
45. Th. Culpeper, *Morall Discourses and Essayes*, London, 1655, p. 63.
46. Thomas Sprat, *The History of the Royal Society of London*, 4th ed., London, 1734, p. 370.

SECTION B

1. Quite apart from exegetical principles, it is evident that in the interpretation of texts concerning the Eucharist, the Reformed Churchmen were less literalistic than the adherents of transubstantiation. On the other hand, the statements made in the Gospels about Jesus' brothers were not taken in the literal sense by Roman Catholic exegetes, who started from the assumption that Mary remained a virgin. The literalistic interpretation of biblical texts was the main argument for Galileo's condemnation; the deviation from Aristotelian philosophy came second.
2. Galileo to Cristina di Lorena (1615), with reference to Tertullian and Augustine; Galileo to Benedetto Castelli, 21-XII-1613. See below, pp. 124 ff.
3. Robert Bellarmine to Paolo Antonio Foscarini: 12-IV-1615.
4. Ecclesiastes 3:10. J. Wilkins, *Discourse concerning a new Planet* (1640), prop. II.

5. Cf. R. Hooykaas, *Humanisme, science et réforme*, ch. xiv ('Ramus, Paracelse, et la Theologia Prisca'), pp. 108-112.

6. Fr. Bacon, *Advancement of Learning*, II. To look for science in the Bible creates not only a *philosophia phantastica*, but also a *religio haeretica* (Bacon, *Novum Organum*, I, aph. LXV). J. Kepler, *Apologia contra Fludd* (1622). J. Wilkins, *Discourse concerning a new Planet* (1640), prop. IV, fin.

7. J. Calvin, *Commentaries on the First Book of Moses, called Genesis* (1554), ch. I, 15. *Commentary on the Psalmes* (1557), Psalm 19:4-6; Psalm 24:2.

8. Calvin, *Institutes*, II. 2. 15.

9. Calvin, *Comment. Genesis* I, 16.

10. Calvin, *Comment. Genesis* I. 6.

11. Calvin, *Comment. Genesis* I. 15; see below, p. 123.

12. Calvin, *Comment. on the Psalmes*, LVIII. 4-5.

13. The possibility that it was the ancient writer's own world picture was not taken into account. However, the difference in sophistication between a naive world picture and naive observation is not great.

14. Calvin, *Comment. Genesis* I. 7.

15. Calvin, *Comment. II Timothy* 3:16.

16. Calvin, *Comment. Romans* 5:15.

17. Calvin, *Comment. I Corinthians* 1:17.

18. Calvin, *Comment. Galatians* 5:11.

19. 1 Corinthians 11:14: 'Does not even nature itself teach you that, if a man have long hair, it is a shame unto him?'

20. Calvin, *Comment. I Corinthians* 11:14.

21. In the Acts of the Apostles, Luke wrote that seventy-five people went with Jacob to Egypt (Acts 7:14), but Deuteronomy 10:22 and Genesis 24:27 mention only seventy. Calvin attributed this to an error of transcription in the Greek version, to which Luke perhaps conformed because people had got accustomed to it; or, perhaps, there was the right number in the original text, but somebody else adapted it to the current version of the Old Testament (*Comment. on Acts* 7:14; Corp. Ref. LXXV). Calvin added, that we should, however, rather concentrate on the miraculous increase of the Jewish people than anxiously bother about one word that changed a number. In his opinion, when Luke says that the patriarchs were laid in the sepulchre that Abraham bought from the sons of Hamor (Acts 7:16), 'he is evidently mistaken', for *Abraham* bought a cave from Ephron the Hittite, in which Jacob was buried (Genesis 50:13), whereas *Jacob* bought a field from the sons of Hamor (Genesis 33:19), and Joseph was buried in that field (Joshua 24:32).

22. Calvin, *Comment. on Acts*, 7:16.

23. See above p. 115.

24. A. D. White, *A History of the Warfare of Science with Theology in Christendom*, London 1896.

25. White, *op. cit.*, p. 127.

26. F. W. Farrar, *History of Interpretation*, London, 1886, p. xviii: ' "Who," asks Calvin, "will venture to place the authority of Copernicus above that of the Holy Spirit?" '

27. R. Hooykaas, '*Thomas Digges' Puritanism*', in: Arch. Internat. Hist. Sciences, 8 (1955), p. 151; '*Science and Reformation*', in: J. World Hist. 3 (1956), pp. 136–138; Revue Hist. Sc. 8 (1955), p. 180.

28. 'But the greatest exegete and theologian of the Reformation was undoubtedly Calvin' (Farrar, *op. cit.*, p. 342); 'he is one of the greatest interpreters of Scripture who ever lived' (*op. cit.*, p. 343); 'A characteristic feature of Calvin's exegesis is its abhorrence of hollow orthodoxy' (p. 345); 'His robust honesty', not accommodating to age-old prejudice, 'drew on him the most savage hatred' of Lutheran and Roman-Catholic theologians (*op. cit.*, p. 346). We might add that, in fact, two great scientists who were accused of "crypto-calvinism" by their Lutheran fellow-believers followed the same exegetical principles as Calvin. The Hamburg physicist Joachim Jungius was persecuted because of his demonstration of "hebraisms" in New Testament Greek; and Kepler had to suffer for his mild attitude towards the Reformed interpretation of Holy Supper.

29. Farrar, *op. cit.*, p. xviii ' "Newton's discoveries", says the Puritan John Owen, "are against evident testimonies of Scripture".'. Further on (*op. cit.* p. 432, n. 2) Farrar gives the place: 'When John Owen (Works, XIX, p. 310) said that Newton's discoveries were "built on fallible phenomena, and advanced by many arbitrary presumptions, against evident testimonies of Scripture", his sentences may stand as but one specimen of hundreds and thousands of the obscurantist utterances of theologians who attribute infallibility to their own exegetical errors'.

Apart from the exaggeration of the accusation against Owen, this quotation, though not wholly fictitious (as was the passage attributed to Calvin), is misleading. In fact, Owen, after mentioning the order of the planets according to the ancient system, continued: 'What alteration is made herein by the late hypothesis fixing the sun as the centre of the world, built on fallible phenomena, and advanced by many arbitrary presumptions, against evident testimonies of Scripture . . . is here of no consideration'. Newton is not mentioned, and it would indeed have been strange if he were, for Owen's work is dated 1671, whereas Newton's *Principia* was published in 1687, that is after Owen's death.

30. Luther, *Tischreden*, Weimar, 1916, vol. 4, nr. 4638, d.d. 4 Juni 1539:

De novo quodam astrologo fiebat mentio. . . . Wer do will klug sein, der soll ihme nichts lassen gefallen das andere achten; er mus ihme etwas eigen machen, *sicut ille facit, qui totam astrologiam invertere vult. Etiam illa confusa tamen ego credo sacrae scripturae, nam Josua iussit solem stare, non terram.*' A later version gives the addition: 'the fool wants to turn upside down the whole of the art of astronomy' (1566). Cf. H. Bornkamm, '*Copernicus im Urteil der Reformation*'. Arch. f. Ref. Gesch., 40 (1943), p. 171 ff.

31. Melanchthon, *Initia doctrinae physicae* (1549). Corp. Ref. XIII. 216 ff.

32. The oration was delivered by Caspar Reinhold. Corp. Ref. XV, col. 833–841.

33a. Corp. Ref. IV, 810, 839.

33b. William Gilbert, *De magnete*, Londini, 1600. Praefatio (by Edw. Wright), fol. Vr.

34. J. Calvin, *Comment. Psalms*, 136:7. See above, p. 118.

35. Quotation from Paul's Epistle to Timothy (2 Timothy 3:16).

36. 1 Kings 7:23; 2 Chronicles 4:2.
   Philippus Lansbergen, *Bedenckingen op den dagelijckschen ende Iaerlijck-schen loop van den Aardkloot* (1st ed., Middelburg, 1629); Middelburg, 1650, pp. 17–22. Latin edition: *Commentationes in motum terrae diurnum et annuum*, Middelburg, 1660. Controversia prima de motu diurno.

37. Jacobus Lansbergius, *Apologia pro Commentationibus Philippi Lansbergii*, Middelburgi Zelandiae, 1633, pp. 49–55.

38. J. Kepler, *Astronomia Nova* (1609). Introductio: 'Holy Scriptures speak about common things (for the instruction in which they have not been instituted) with human beings in a human way, so that they may be understood by mankind; they use what is generally acknowledged by men, in order to bring home to them other things, more lofty and divine'. The intention of Genesis 1 is, in Kepler's opinion, to exalt the known things, and not to inquire into the unknown things. Cf. J. Kepler, *Tertius interveniens* (1610), theses VII; LIV, 4.

39. Galileo to Castelli, 21-XII-1613; Galileo to the Grand-Duchess Christina.

40. Galileo to Elia Diodati, 15-I-1633.

41. Galileo to Piero Dini, 23-III-1615; Galileo to Leopold of Austria, 23-V-1618.

42. Galileo to Castelli, 14-XII-1613; to Grand-Duchess Christina (1615).

43. Galileo to Dini, 23-III-1615. Galileo's exposition is based on the text of the Vulgate, Ps. 18:6, 8: *In sole posuit tabernaculum suum: et ipse tanquam sponsus procedens de thalamo suo: Exultavit ut gigas ad currendam viam . . . A summo coelo egressio ejus: Et occursus ejus usque ad summum ejus; nec est qui se abscondet a calore ejus. Lex Domini immaculata convertens animas.* . . .

44. J. Wilkins, *Discovery of a New World* (1638), prop. II; *Discourse concerning a New Planet* (1640), prop. III.
45. Wilkins, *Discovery*, prop. II.
46. Wilkins, *Discourse*, prop. IV: 'That divers Learned Men have fallen into great Absurdities, whilst they have looked for the Sects of Philosophy from the Words of Scripture.'
47. Wilkins, *Discovery*, prop. IX.
48. Wilkins, *Discourse*, prop. II.
49. J. Kepler, *Astronomia Nova; Introductio.*
50. Wilkins, *Discovery*, prop. III.
51. R. F. Jones, *The Seventeenth Century*, Stanford, 1951[1], 1965[2], p. 155.
52. Wilkins, *Discourse*, prop. II, I.
53. Jos. 10:12. Wilkins, *Discourse*, prop. II.
54. Wilkins, *Discourse*, prop. II, 2, 30.
55. Wilkins, *Discourse*, prop. II.
56. Wilkins, *Discourse*, prop. VII, fin.
57. Wilkins, *Discourse*, prop. X.
58. Wilkins, *Discourse* (1640), title-page.
59. Wilkins, *Discovery* (1638), title-page.
60. See above, pp. 126 ff. (Wilkins) and 123 (Lansbergen).
61. G. Voetius, *Sermoen van de Nuttigheydt der Academien*, Utrecht, 1636, pp. 35-36.
62. Robert Bellarmine to P. A. Foscarini, 12-IV-1615.
63. G. Voetius, *Thersites heautontimoroumenos*, Ultrajecti 1635, pp. 266, 281, 283.
64. G. Voetius, *Disputationes selectae*, vol. I, Ultrajecti 1648, p. 552 (de creatione); *Thersites*, p. 256.
65. N. Carpenter, *Geographie delineated forth*, Bk. I, ch. iv.
66. Galileo to Federico Cesi, 8-VI-1624.
67. Galileo to Francesco Ingoli (answer to the latter's *Disputatio de situ et quiete terrae contra Copernici systema*, 1616), 1624.
68. Galileo's Letter to Grand-Duchess Christina, 1615.
69. B. Pascal, *Lettres provinciales*, XVIII, *au père Annat, S.J.*, 24-III-1657. Cf. R. Hooykaas, *Pascal, his Science and his Religion*, in: Free Univ. Qu. 2 (1952), pp. 113; 115.

SECTION C

1. Cf. R. Hooykaas, *Thomas Digges' Puritanism*, in: Arch. intern. hist. sc. 8 (1955), p. 155.
2. Thomas Digges' cousin and namesake distinguished in a pamphlet of 1601 between '*protestants*, viz. such as depend upon ecclesiastical dignities', and '*puritans*, viz. such as pretend perfection in religion'. 'Now this word *Calvinists* comprehendeth *Protestants* as well as

Puritans'. He believed that every sincere Protestant was more or less a Puritan: 'We are all puritans in hart'. Cf. Arch. intern. hist. sc. 8, p. 157.
3. See above, Ch. V, p. 116.
4. They showed affinity with Quakers as well as with Latitudinarians (J. D. Roberts, *From Protestantism to Platonism in Seventeenth-century England*, The Hague, 1968, pp. 216, 230, 232). Cambridge Platonism arose in puritan Emmanuel College (Roberts, *op. cit.*, p. 256). One of the Cambridge Platonists' favourite texts was: 'The reason of Man is the candle of the Lord' (Proverbs 20:27). In how far they deviated from the Puritan line was clearly exposed by A. Tuckney (*None but Christ*, Cambridge, 1654, pp. 50–51), when saying: 'I would not have that candle put out, I would have it snuffed and improved as a hand-maid to faith . . . not that candle light but the Sun of Righteousness, that will guide our feet into the way of peace' (Roberts, *op. cit.*, p. 65). This is again the inevitable problem of 'reason' and 'nature', which so much occupied Pascal, Boyle, *et al.* in the seventeenth century and the Nominalists in the fourteenth.
5. C. S. Lewis, *English Literature in the Sixteenth Century, excluding Drama*, Oxford, 1954, p. 43.
   According to Tawney, 'where Catholic and Anglican had caught a glimpse of the invisible, hovering like a consecration over the gross world of sense, and touching its muddy vesture with the unearthly gleam of a divine, yet familiar, beauty, the Puritan moaned for a lost Paradise and creation sunk in sin' (R. H. Tawney, *Religion and the Rise of Capitalism*, London, 1938, p. 228). This verdict has only rhetorical value. Evidently, Lewis and Tawney, though being of the same High Church (non-Puritan) persuasion, did not possess the faculty of sympathetic imagination to the same degree.
6. J. Spedding, *Introduction to Bacon's Religious Writings*, in: *Works of Francis Bacon*, vol. VII.
7. D. Stimson, in: Isis 23 (1935), p. 374.
8. John Hall, *An Humble Motion to the Parliament of England concerning the Advancement of Learning and the Reformation of the Universities*, London, 1649, p. 21.
9. J. Wilkins, *Mathematicall Magick* (1648), Bk. I, ch. 1.
10. J. Wilkins, *Mercury: or The Secret and Swift Messenger* (1641), ch. xiii.
11. Numbers 11:29, J. Milton, *Areopagitica*.
12. James 1:17, F. Bacon, *Novum Organum* I, aph. 93.
13. Zechariah 14:17.
14. Proverbs 20:27. This was a text cherished by the Cambridge Platonists ('The spirit of man is the Candle of the Lord').
15a. J. A. Comenius, *The Way of Light*.
15b. Cf. Malachi 11:2.

16. John Hall, *op. cit.*, p. 18.

17. R. K. Merton, *op. cit.*, p. 495.

18. It has been said that it is impossible to obtain reliable statistical results on the religious affiliation of scientists in general, whereas it is much easier to obtain them for the separate disciplines, in which case it is possible to indicate the really important ones (F. Russo, S.J., in: J. World Hist. 3 (1957), p. 857). However, the sum of the cultivators of the diverse scientific disciplines is the number of scientists in general. The sociologists have borrowed their information from biographical dictionaries, so that their own bias has largely been eliminated. When choosing the really important ones, however, one easily introduces another subjective factor: who is to be considered not only a scientist but an 'important' scientist, and who is not important? Besides, it should be realized that the quality of the work is irrelevant for establishing the popularity of science. The subjectivity of this method is evident with Russo himself, who praises it so much. For each discipline he finds as many outstanding cultivators among the Roman Catholics as among the Protestants (and he arrives at this remarkable result by omitting, e.g., such important scientists as the astronomer Tycho Brahe). Even if his conclusion—that the numbers of important scientists on both sides are equal—were right, this would only confirm the sociologists' thesis; as the total number of Roman Catholics is so much larger than that of Protestants, equality of numbers of great specialists on both sides would in fact be to the credit of the smaller group.

19. John Wallis to Robert Boyle, 1-VII-1669.

20. Menno Symons, *Bekentenisse en Aenwysinge* (1581). *Met een grondelijke Confutation . . . van Johanne a Lasco tegen ons in zijn Defension opgebraght.* Menno wrote: 'learning and gifts of tongues I have not despised in all my life, but I have honoured and loved them since my youth, though (alas!) I have not acquired them. Thank God, I am not so far out of my mind that I would despise or scorn the science of tongues by which the precious Word of divine grace has come to us.'

21. J. B. Mullinger, *The University of Cambridge*, vol. III, Cambridge, 1911, pp. 447 ff.

22. Mullinger, *op. cit.*, p. 451.

23. Mullinger, *op. cit.*, p. 452.

24. W. Schenk, *The Concern for Social Justice in the Puritan Revolution*, London, 1948, p. 89.

25. Milton, *Address to Parliament* (preface to *Considerations touching the likeliest means to remove Hirelings out of the Church*, London, 1659); cf. Mullinger, *op. cit.*, p. 524.

26. Mullinger, *op. cit.*, p. 454.

27. R. Hooykaas, 'Science and Theology in the Middle Ages', in: Free Univ. Qu.3 (1954), p. 140, pp. 155 ff.
28. Robert Browne, *A treatise upon the 23. of Matthewe . . . for avoyding . . . wicked Preachers and hirelings* (1582): 'Ye have too long doted about words . . . and wearied your selves with your logick fopperies, and fed your selves with the winde . . .' (p. 181).

Browne deemed the study of the arts of Logic and Rhetoric super-fluous not only for divinity, but also for the science of nature: 'For what man which would know a thing, would not seeke out the nature thereof, whereby it worketh, and keepeth itself, which they call the defining Differences: we should seeke out the workes of God, so should we be readie in the kindes and sortes of things, in the Names and Natures which belong unto them. But nowe their logike hath helde them so long in learning what they should do, that they have done little or nothing at all . . .' (p. 179). Browne points out that Solomon, though excelling in wisdom the children of the East, did not excel them in Logic; his way of studying things was 'by minding and pondering them one by one . . . yea by experience especially' (p. 179). In the latter sentence Browne puts the emphasis on the empirical study of individual things, in the spirit of nominalism.

The Brownist Henry Ainsworth, too, manifested a positive attitude towards science and learning; stressing, however, that the wisdom of which Paul speaks, is of a different and higher kind: 'The *learning*, whereof the Apostle speaketh to Timothee, we love and long after, as being the chiefest of all other: namely, the learning of the Scriptures, and of Jesus Christ. Other learning also we *despise not*, but both we have studied and do use it . . . with the *reason* God hath given us, to the furtherance of the truth, for its benefit to others, and glory of God' (*Apologie or Defence of such true Christians as are commonly (but uniustly) called* Brownists . . . *against such imputations as are layd upon them by the Heads and Doctors of the University of Oxford* (1604), p. 116.

29. W. Schenk, *op. cit.*, p. 110. Gerrard Winstanley, in his *The Law of Freedom*, wrote: 'to know the secrets of nature is to know the works of God: and to know the works of God within the Creation, is to know God himself; for God dwells in every visible work or body . . .'. 'Man will come to know the secrets of Nature and Creation, within which all true knowledge is wrapped up; and the light in man must arise to search it out'. Winstanley's religion consists in an intellectual and mystical knowledge of nature; in spite of its unorthodoxy it shows affinity with the tenets of the spiritualistic puritan sects.
30. William Walwyn, *Walwyns Just Defence against the Aspersions cast upon him*, in *A late un-christian Pamphlet entituled, 'Walwyns Wiles'*, London, 1649, pp. 9–10.

31. G. Voetius, *Sermoen van de nuttigheydt der Academien*, Utrecht, 1636, p. 134.
32. R. F. Jones, in: Isis 31 (1939), pp. 65–67.
33. R. K. Merton, *op. cit.*, p. 495.

EPILOGUE

Without claiming any intellectual superiority for the scientists of the Renaissance and Baroque periods over their ancient and medieval European predecessors or over Oriental philosophers, one has to recognize as a simple fact that 'classical modern science' arose only in the western part of Europe in the sixteenth and seventeenth centuries. Once the right methods had been discovered and solid foundations laid, each new development in the fundamental science of nature (physics) refines and corrects, but does not completely overthrow, the older one. Henceforth, from this point on, anyone with the necessary talent may help to build up science on solidly established foundations. Scientists from nations whose own culture did not give birth to anything like western science have already made notable contributions to it. Western people who have lost all contact with the religion of their forebears continue in their scientific activities the tradition inherited from them.

Though now and again materialistic and naturalistic dogmas are put forward as conclusions from scientific results, these claims are hardly more justifiable than the pretensions of some of our ancestors to found theological tenets on a scientific basis. We have tried to show in these pages that the reverse is more likely to have been the real situation: Science is more a consequence than a cause of a certain religious view.

The confrontation of Graeco-Roman culture with biblical religion engendered, after centuries of tension, a new science. This science preserved the indispensable parts of the ancient heritage (mathematics, logic, methods of observation and experimentation), but it was directed by different social and methodological conceptions, largely stemming from a biblical world view. Metaphorically speaking, whereas the bodily ingredients of science may have been Greek, its vitamins and hormones were biblical.

The question may be raised whether this result could not have been brought about in a different way. Of course, logically speaking, when *now* a non-christian world manipulates 'science in the modern sense', this same situation might have been possible in the seventeenth century and other epochs, and also in other places than western Europe. Historically speaking, however, it makes little sense to reconstruct a course of history different from that which actually took place. Things happened thus and therefore, thus they must have happened.